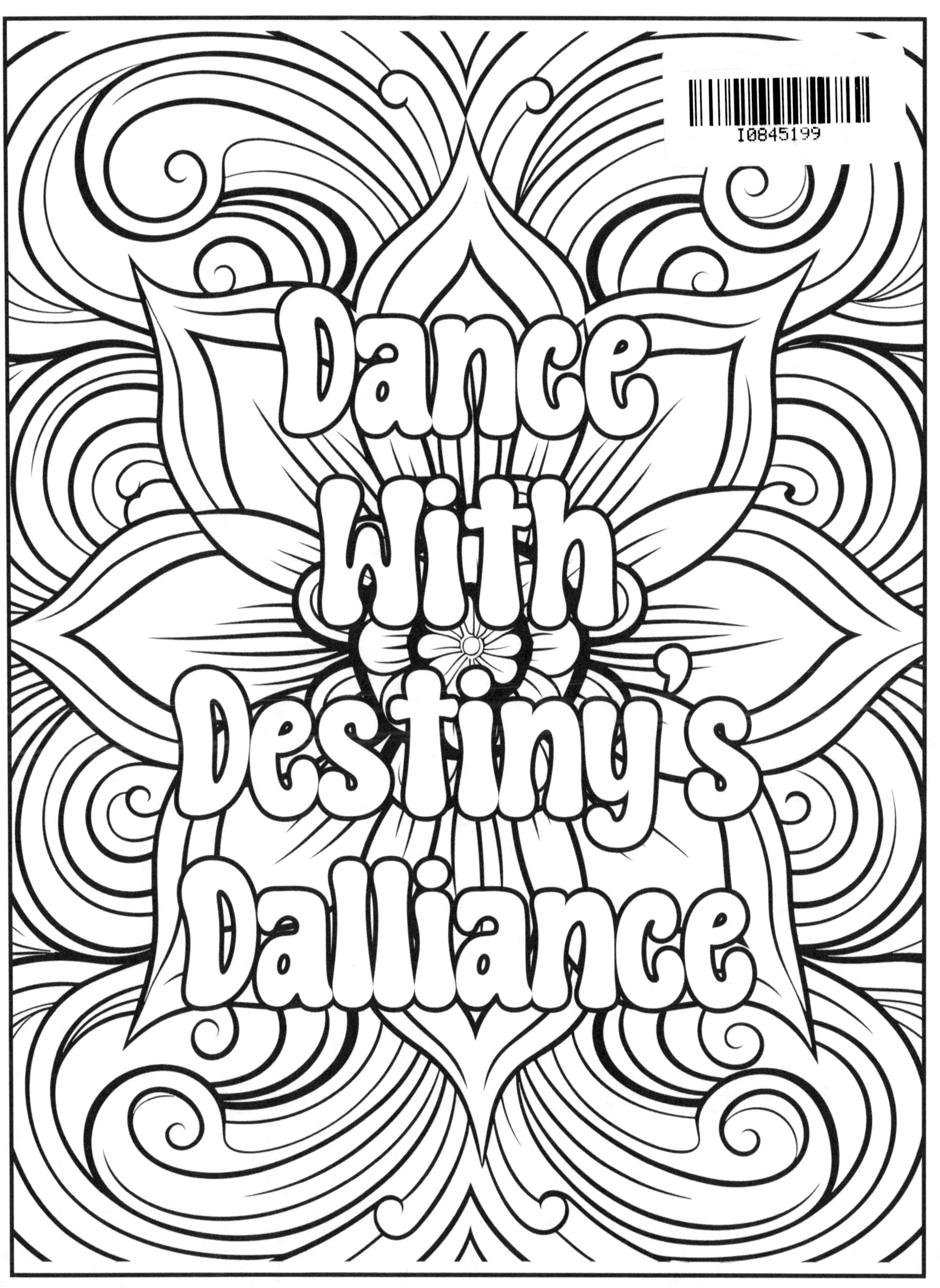
Dance
With
Destiny's
Dalliance

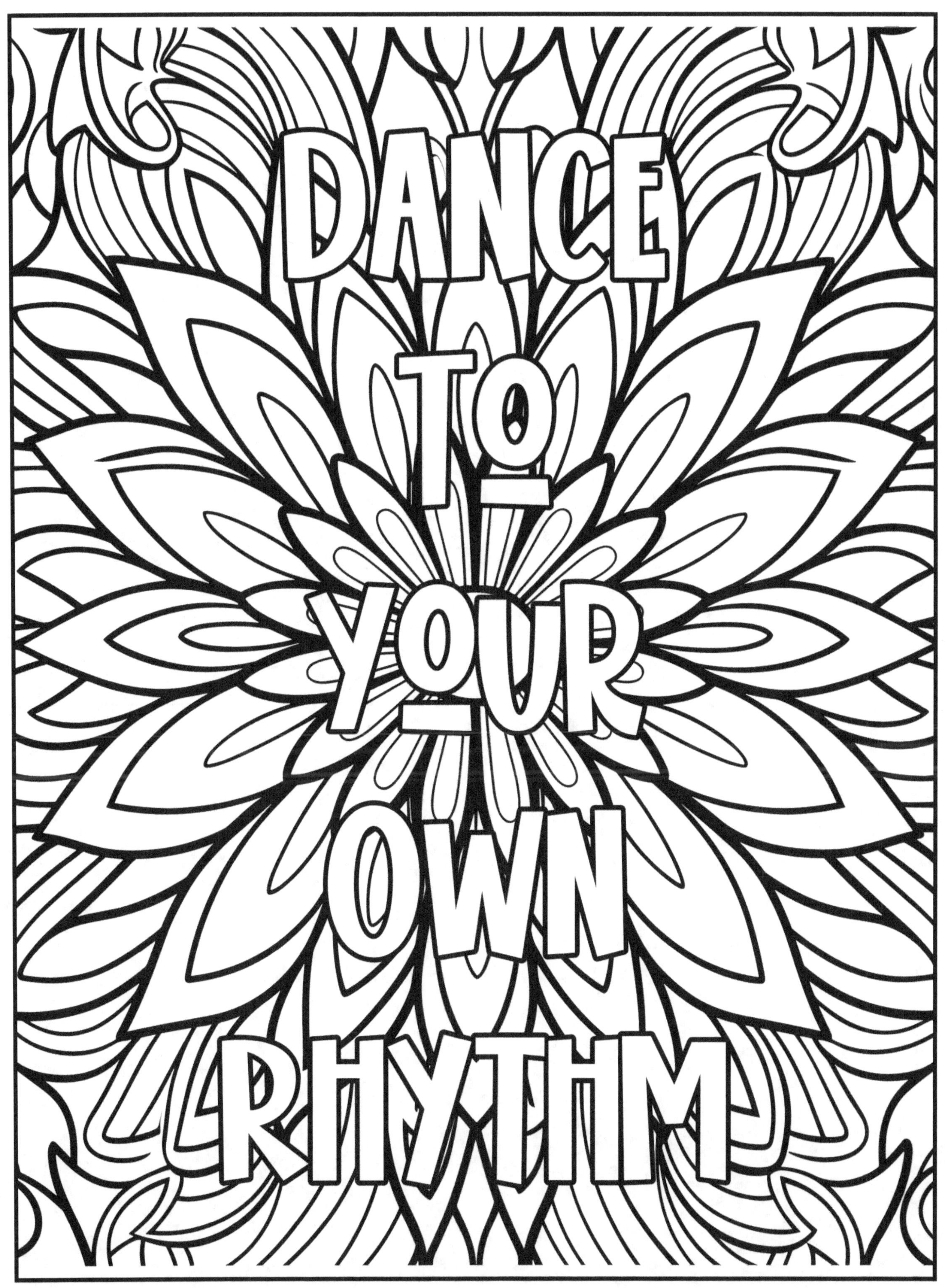
DANCE
TO
YOUR
OWN
RHYTHM

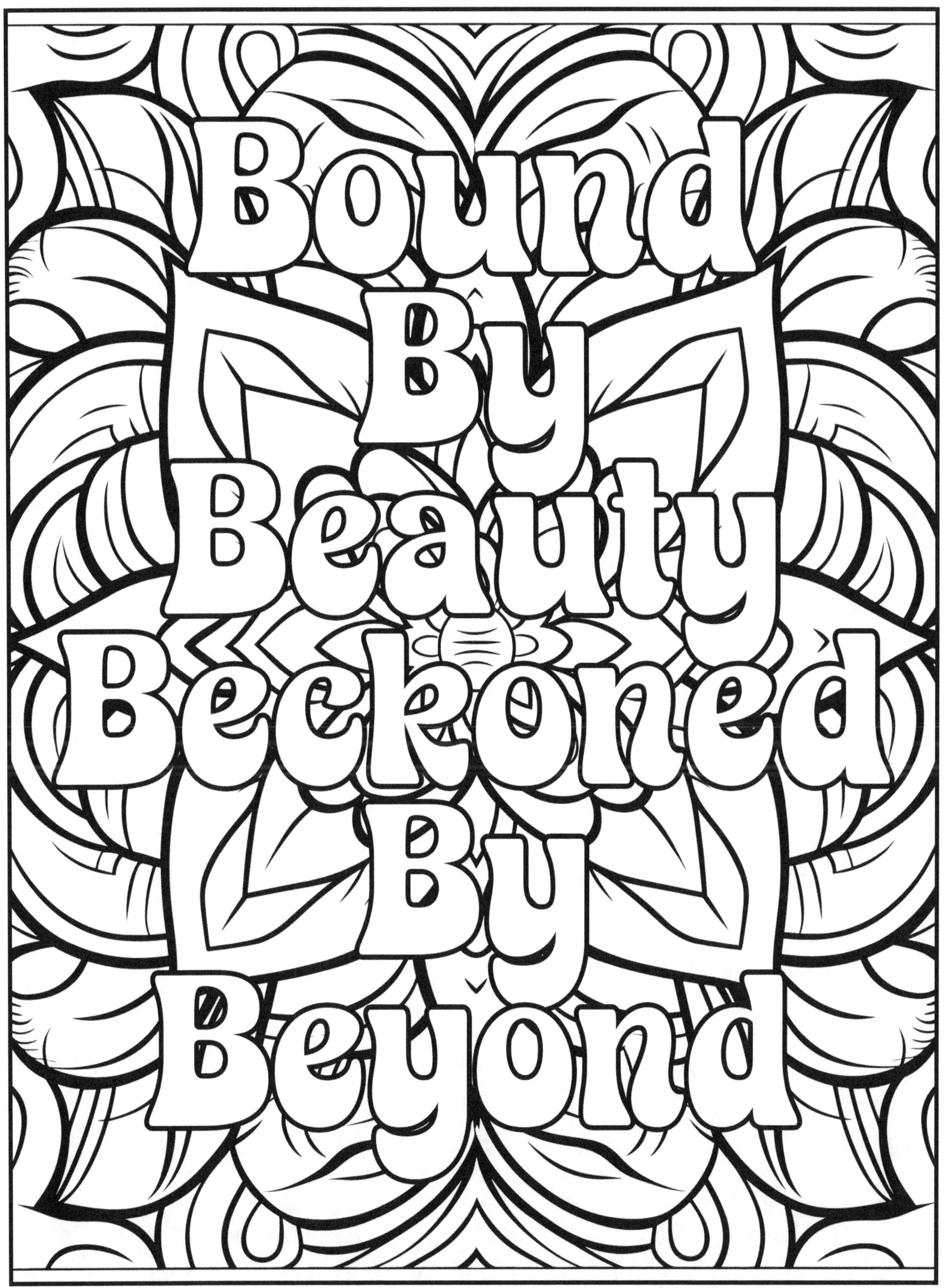

Bound
By
Beauty
Beckoned
By
Beyond

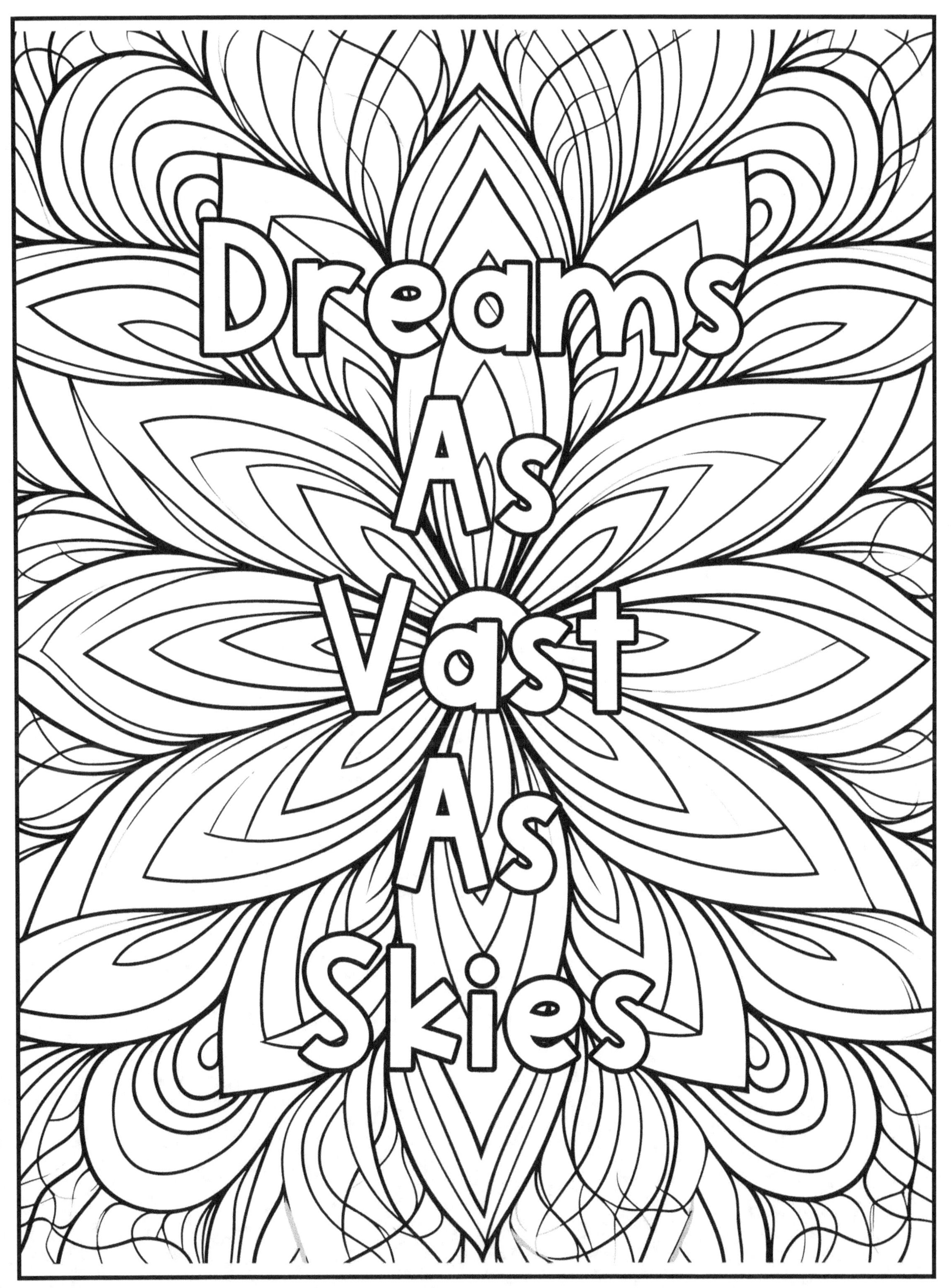

Dreams
As
Vast
As
Skies

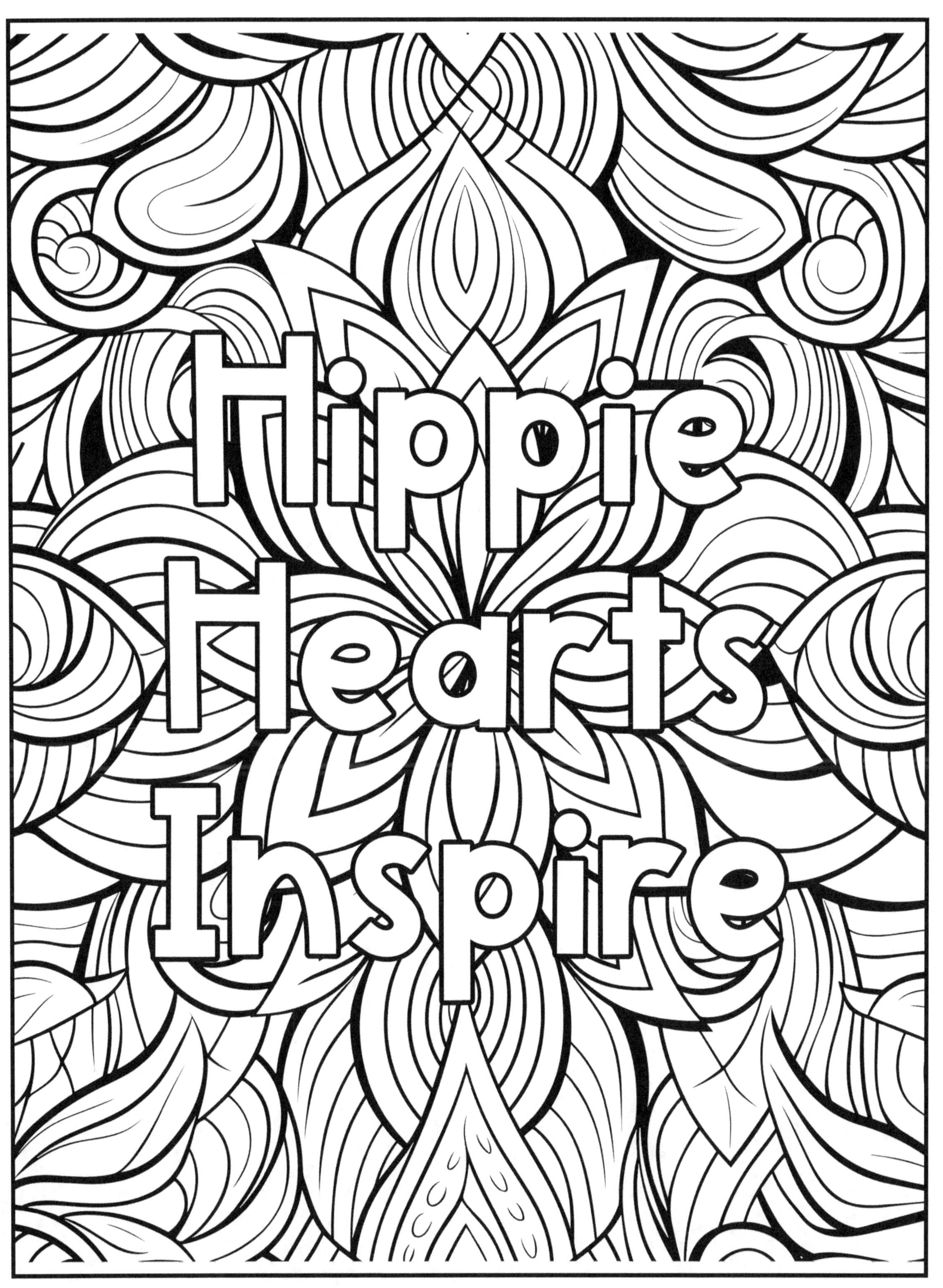

Hippie
Hearts
Inspire

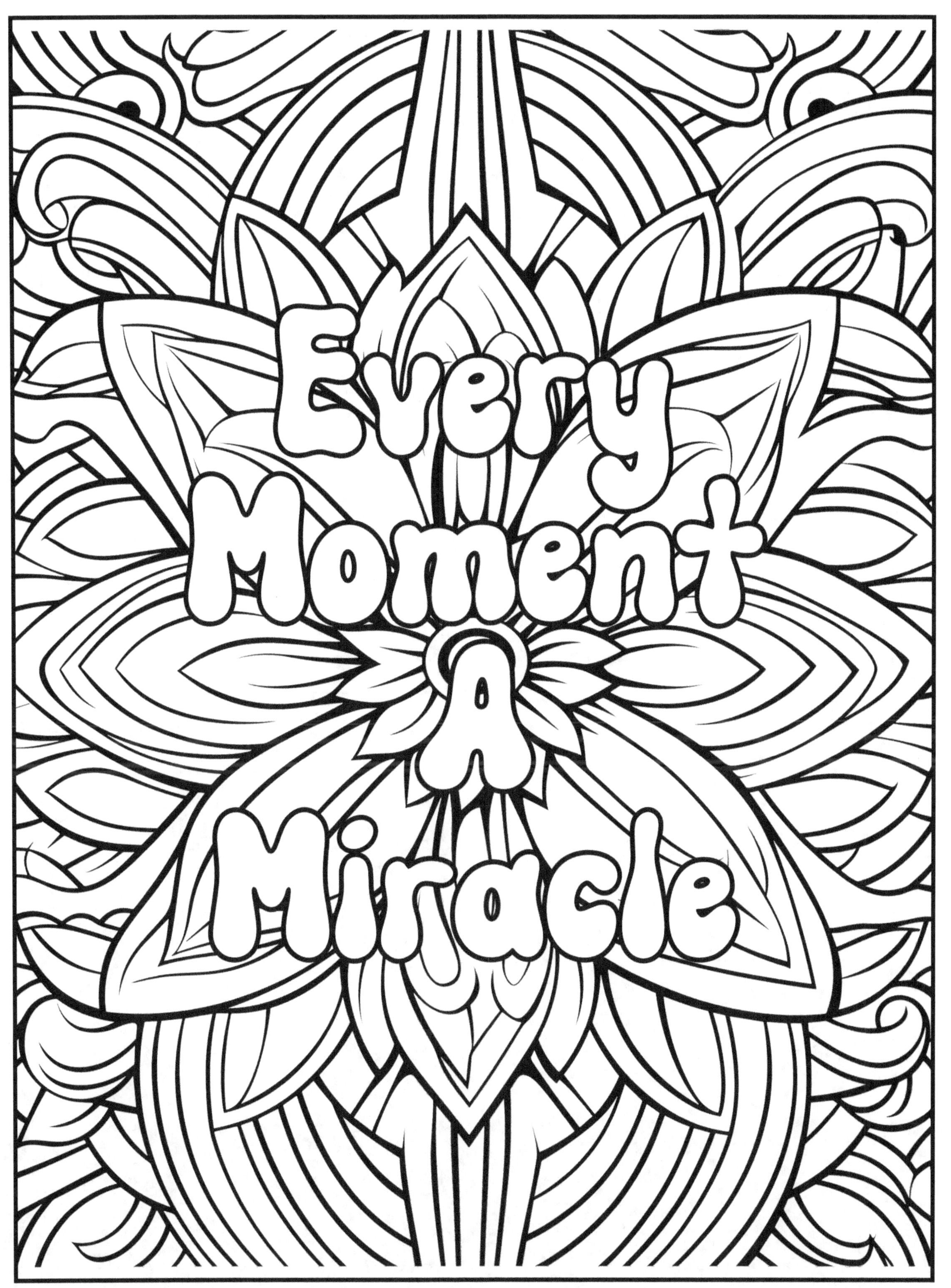

Every
Moment
A
Miracle

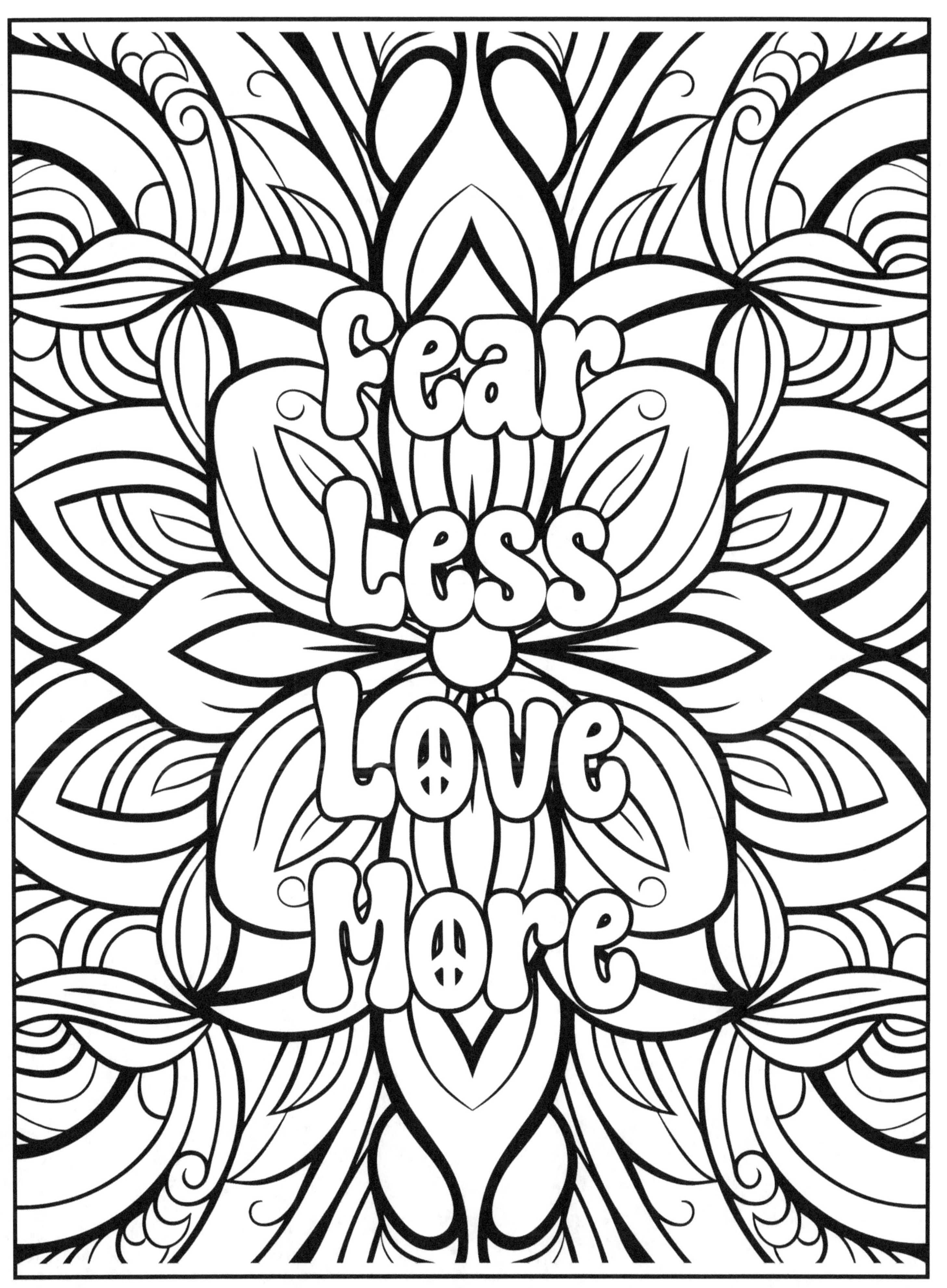

Fear
Less
Love
More

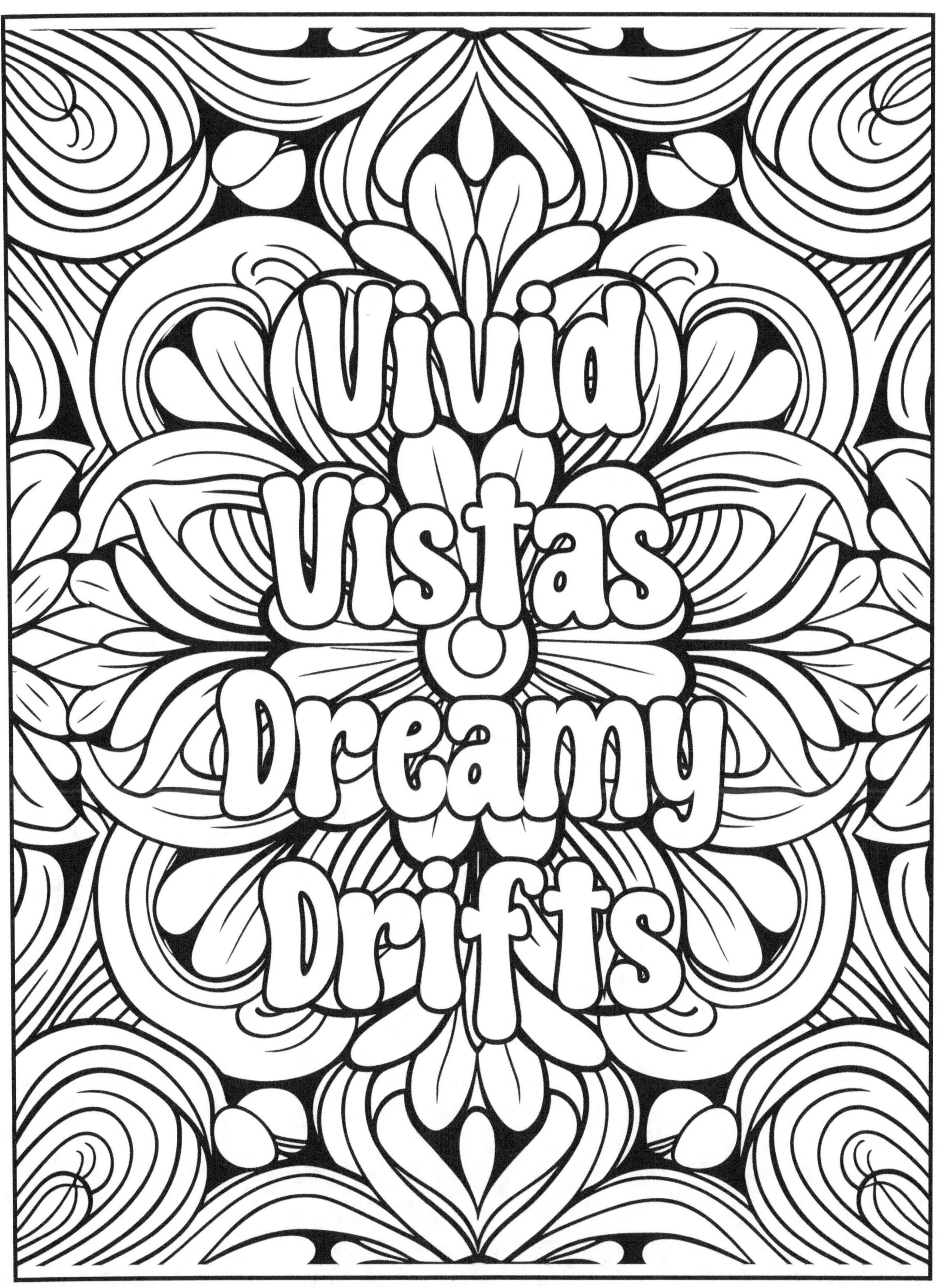

Vivid
Vistas
Dreamy
Drifts

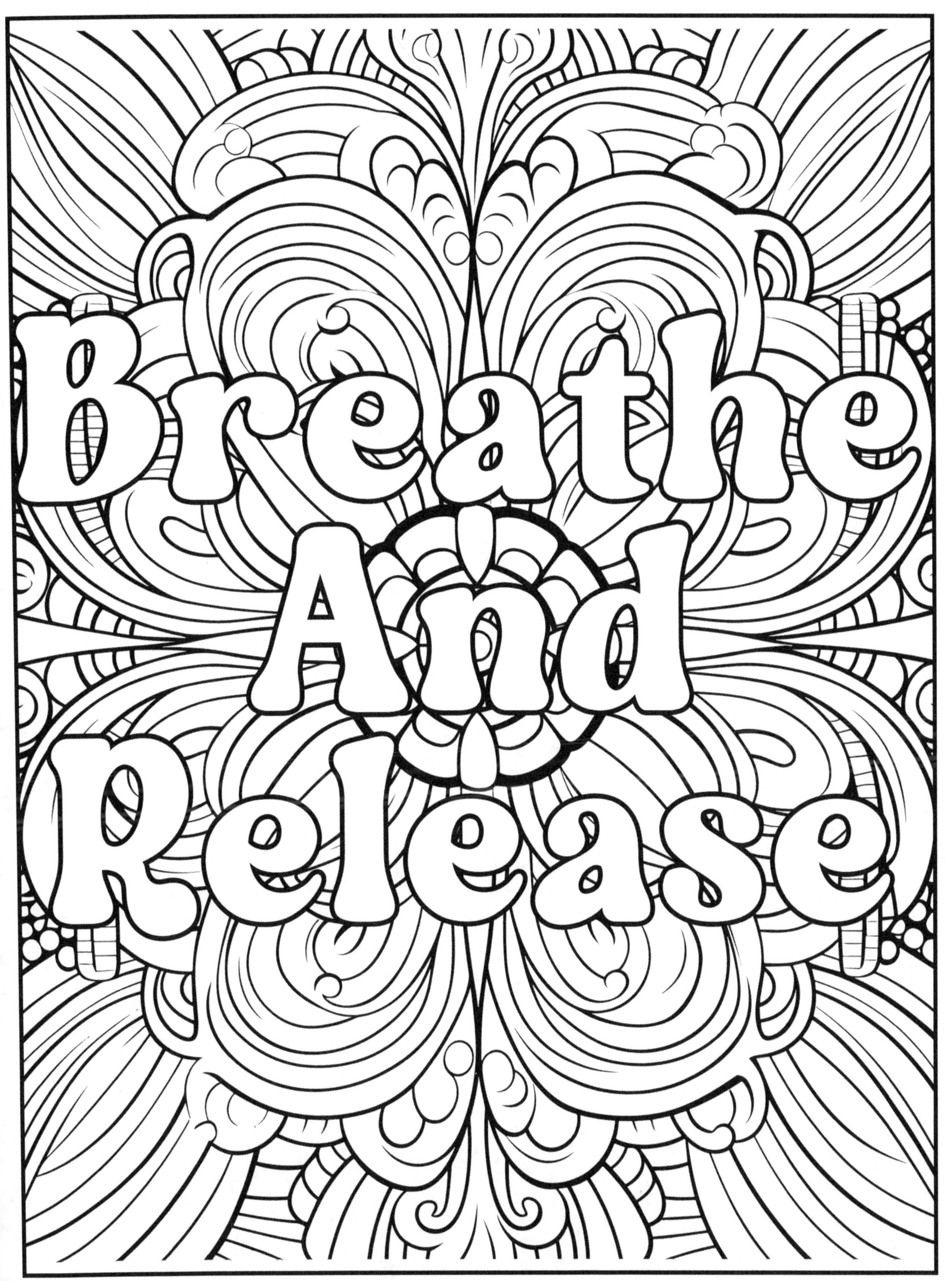

Breathe
And
Release

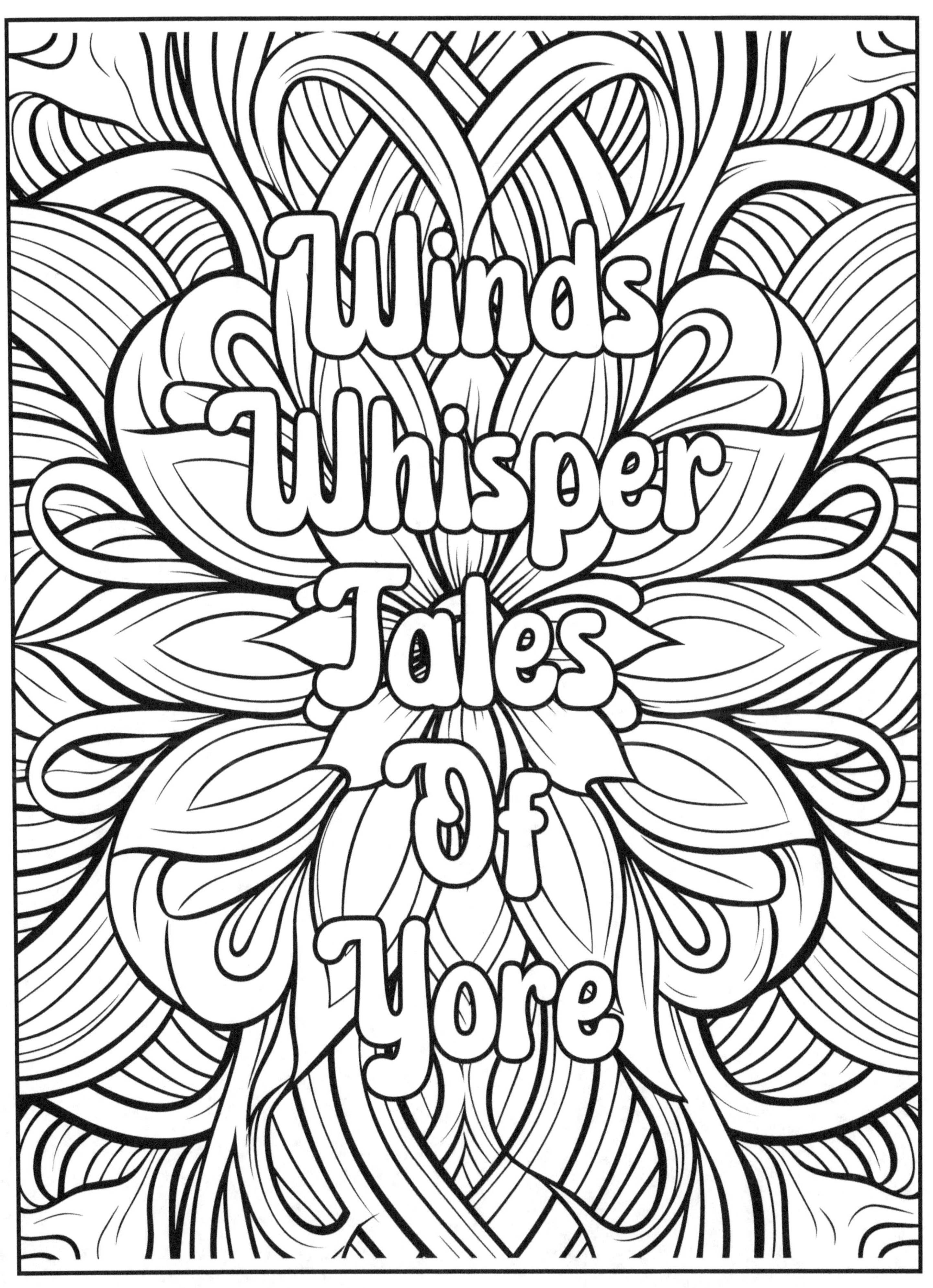

Winds
Whisper
Tales
Of
Yore!

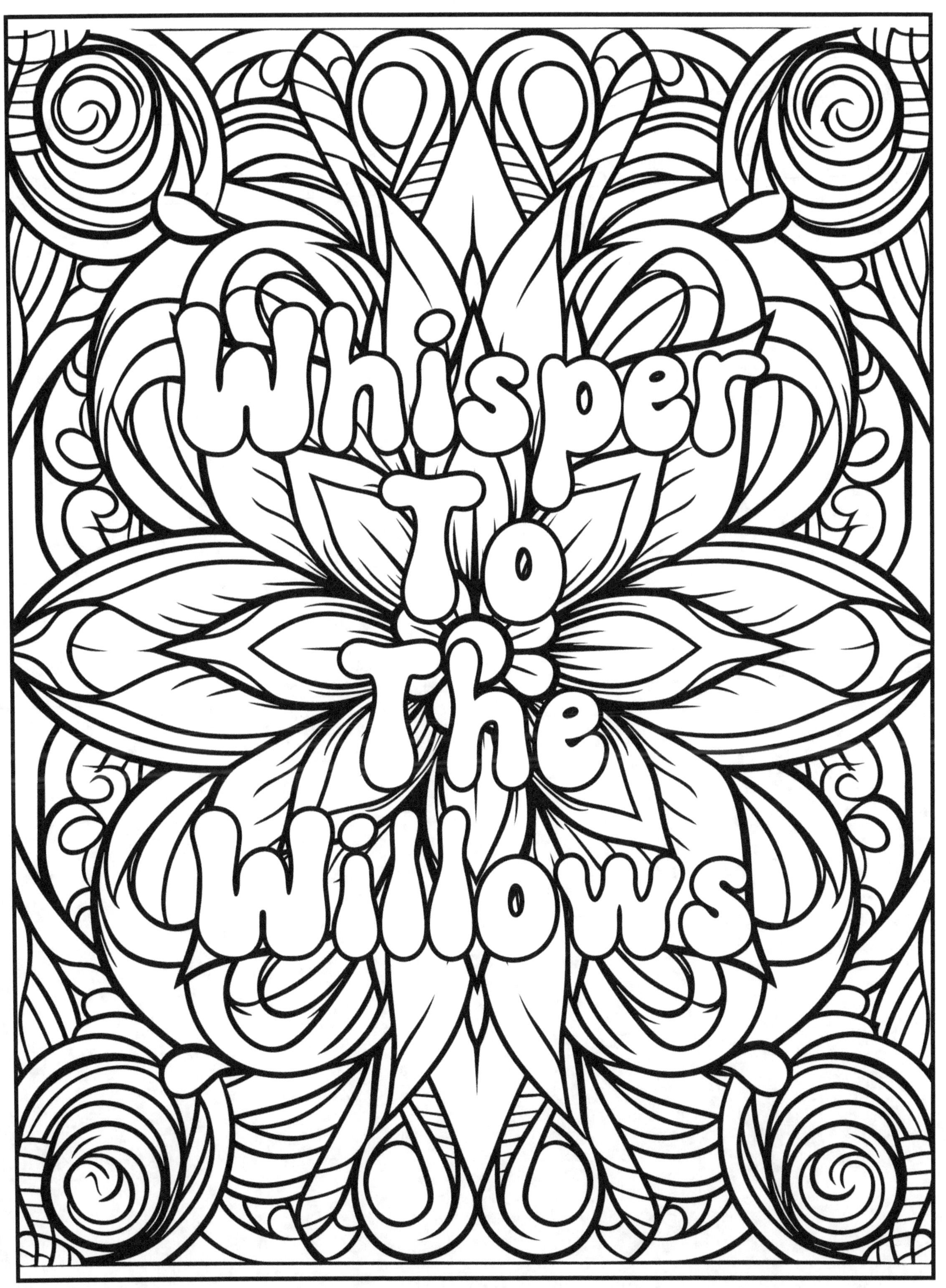

Whisper
To
The
Willows

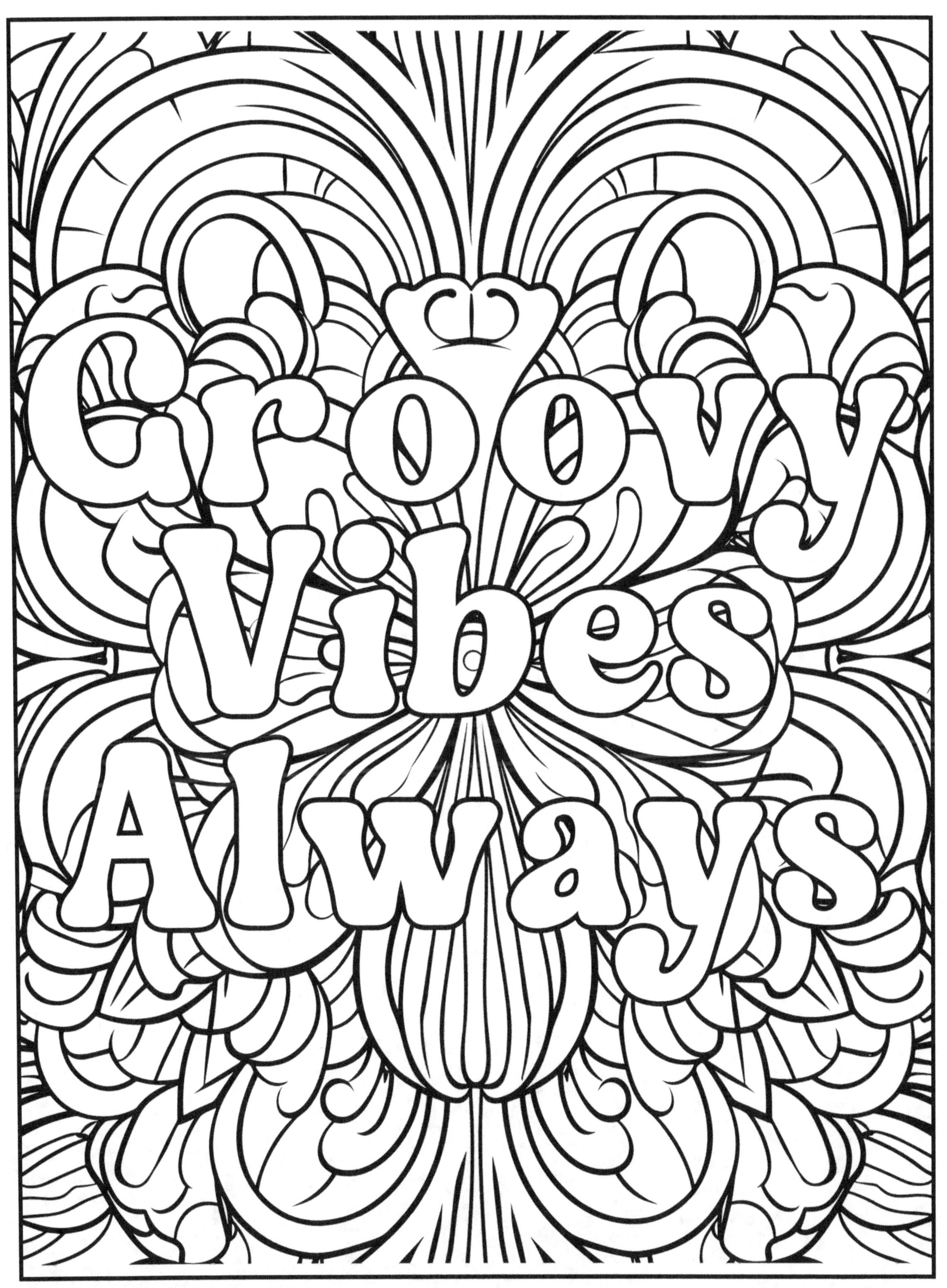

Groovy
Vibes
Always

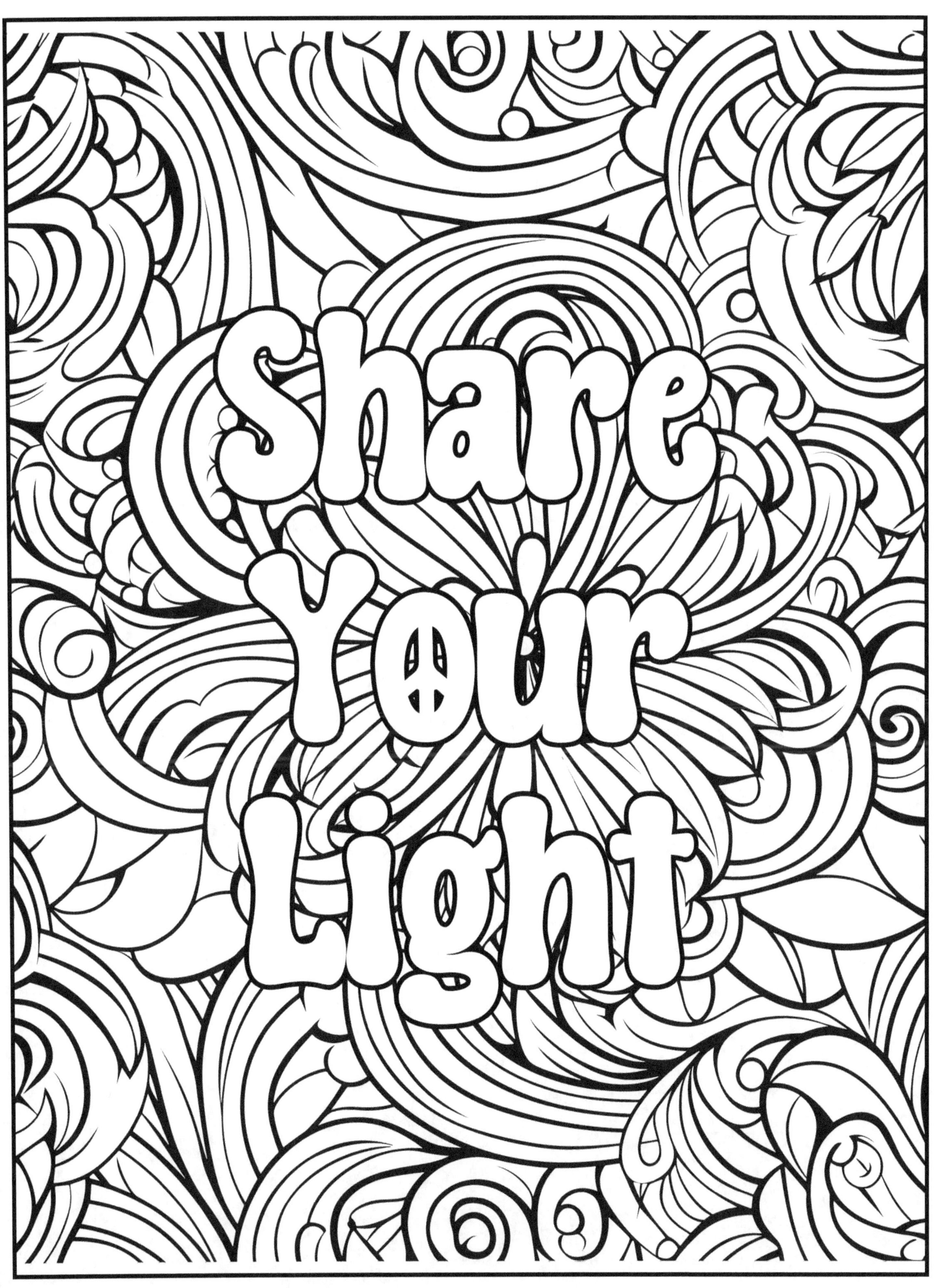

Share
Your
Light

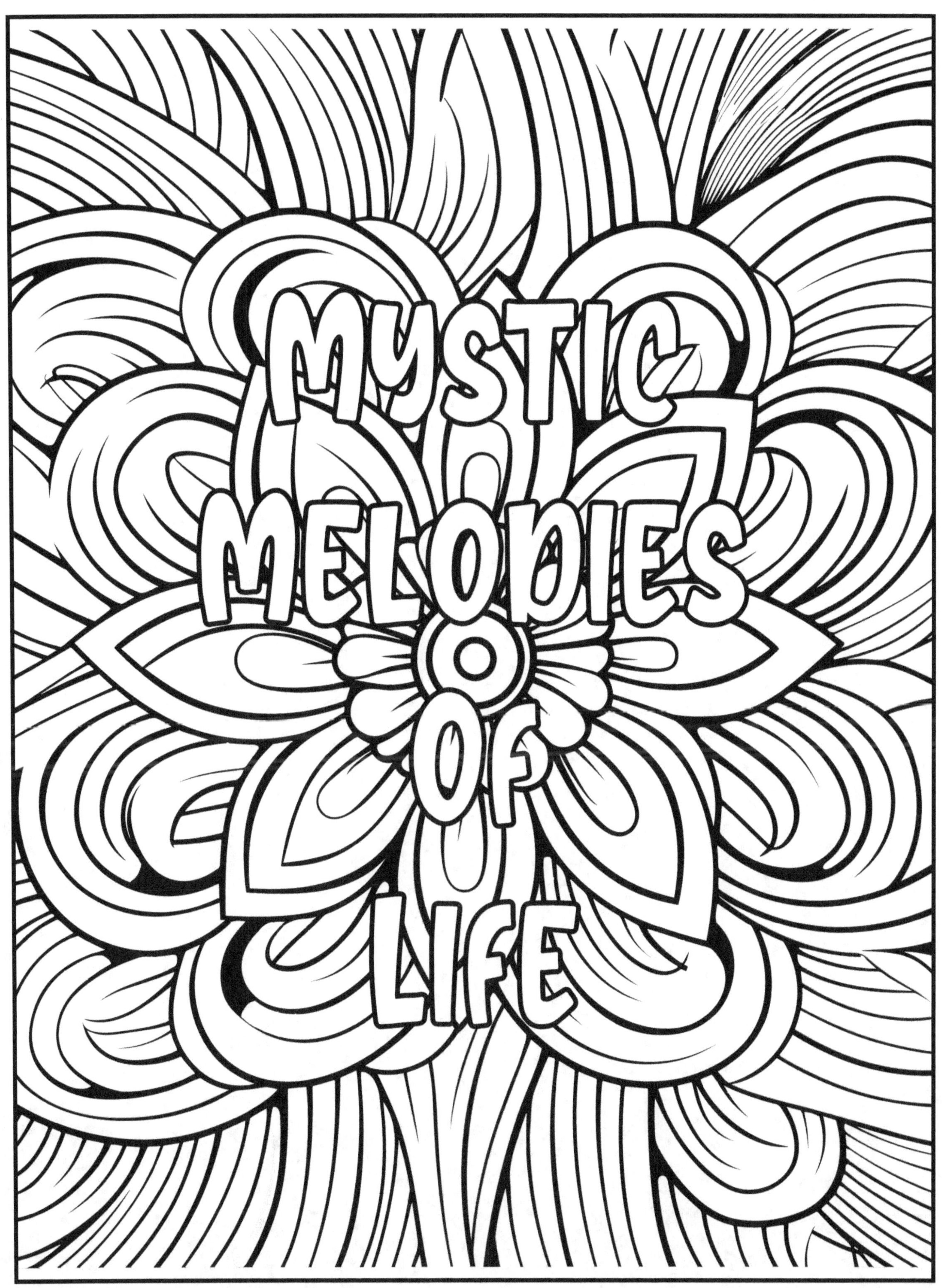

MYSTIC
MELODIES
OF
LIFE

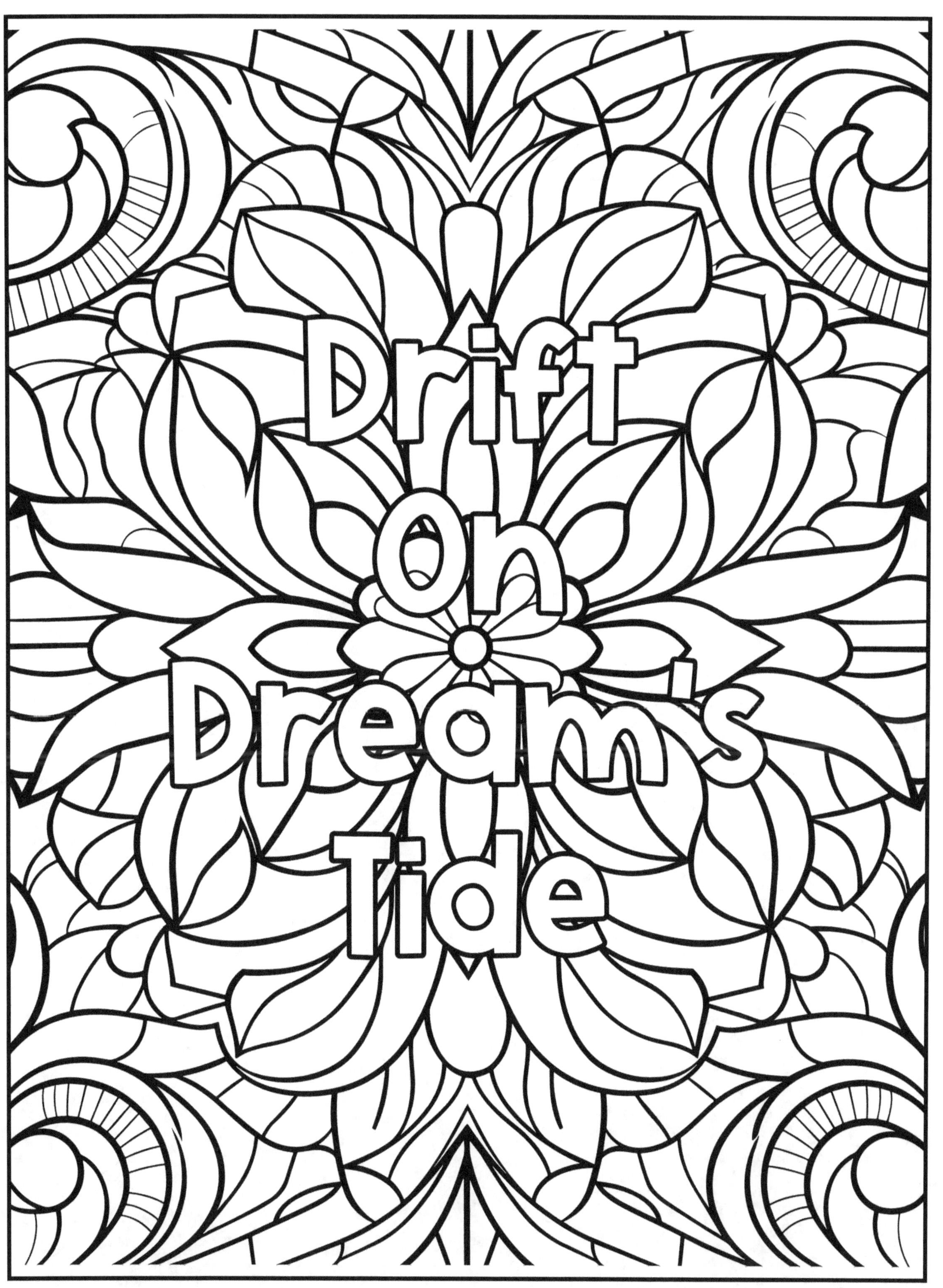
Drift
On
Dream's
Tide

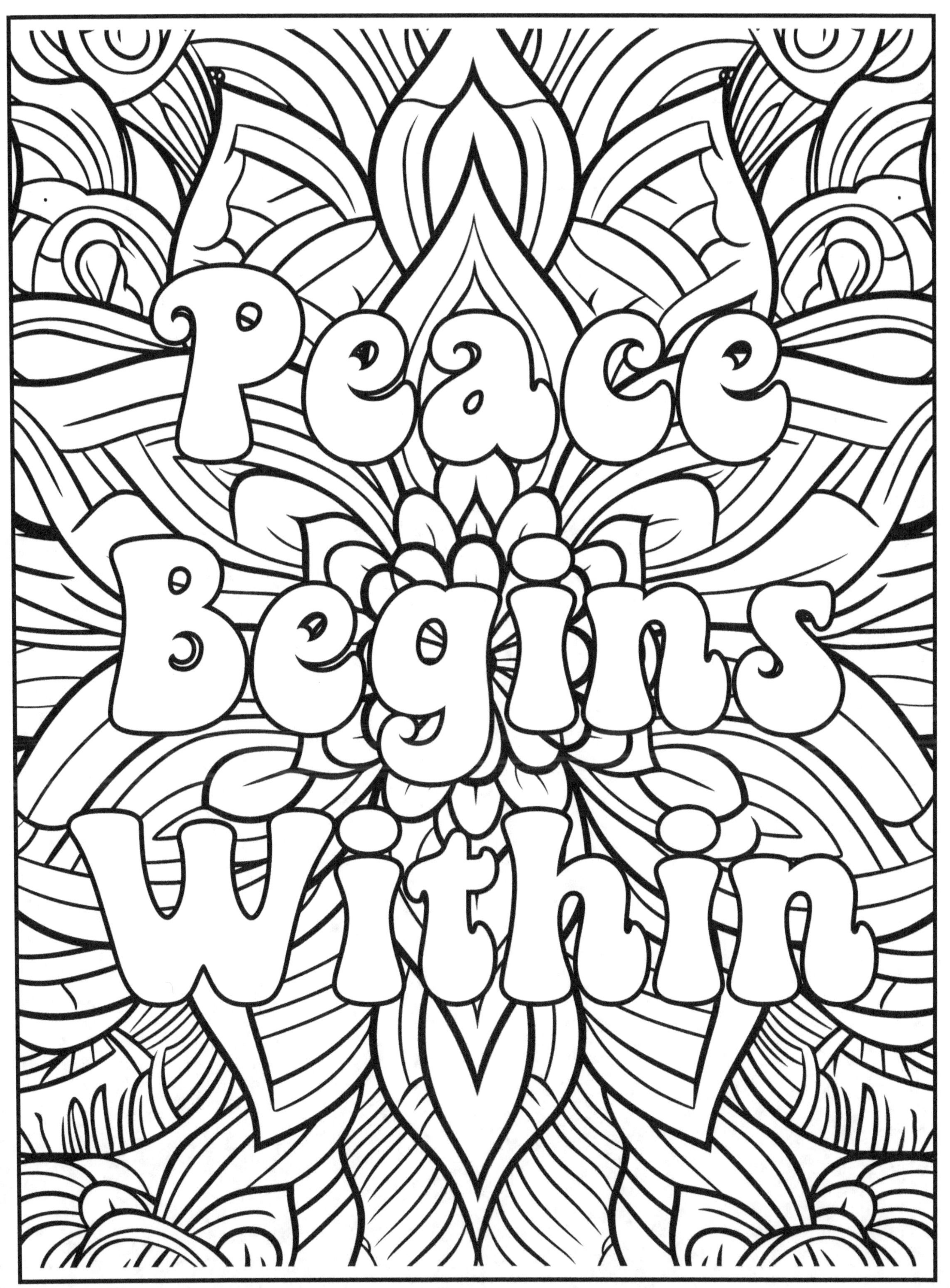

Peace
Begins
Within

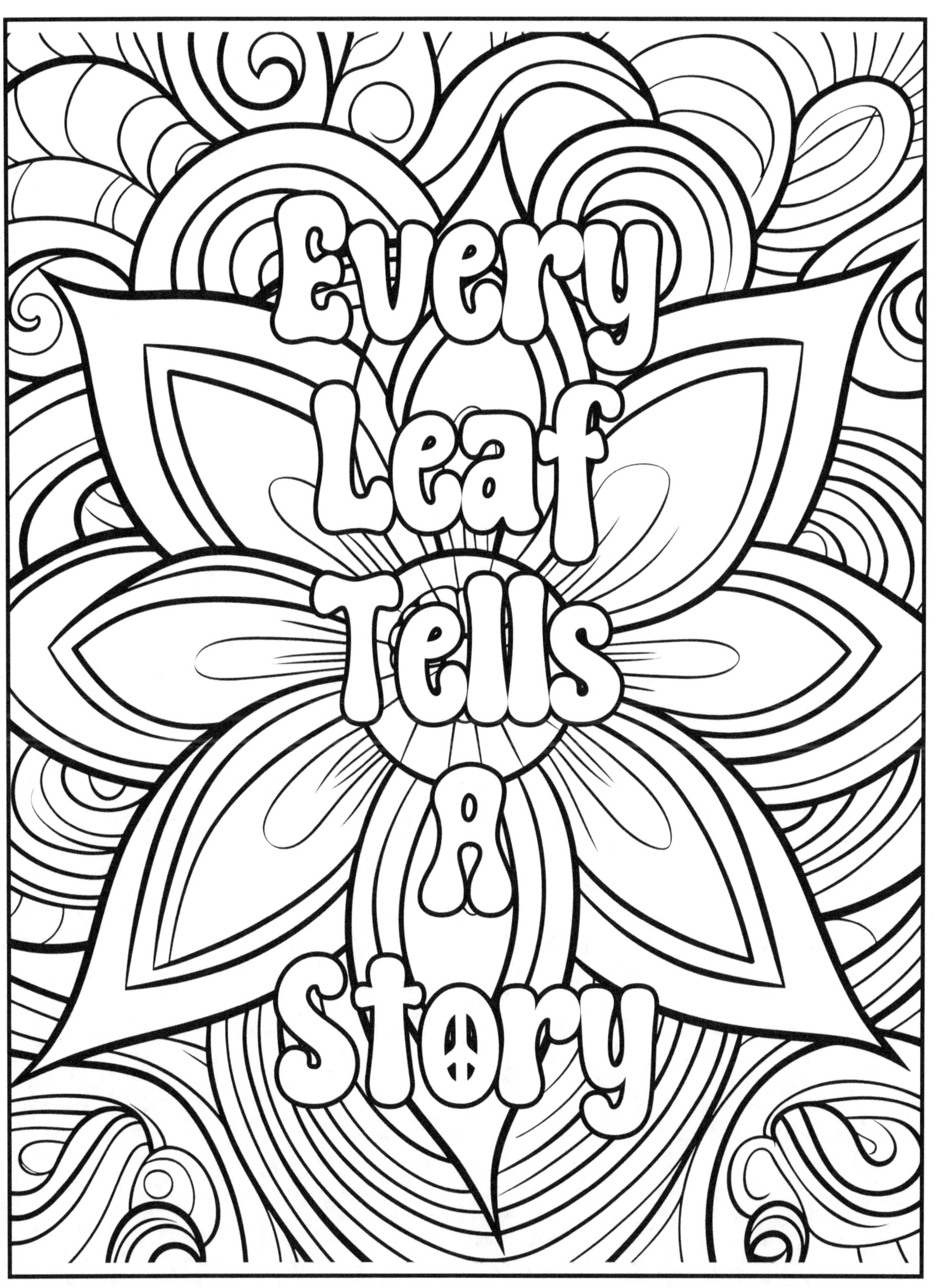

Every
Leaf
Tells
A
Story

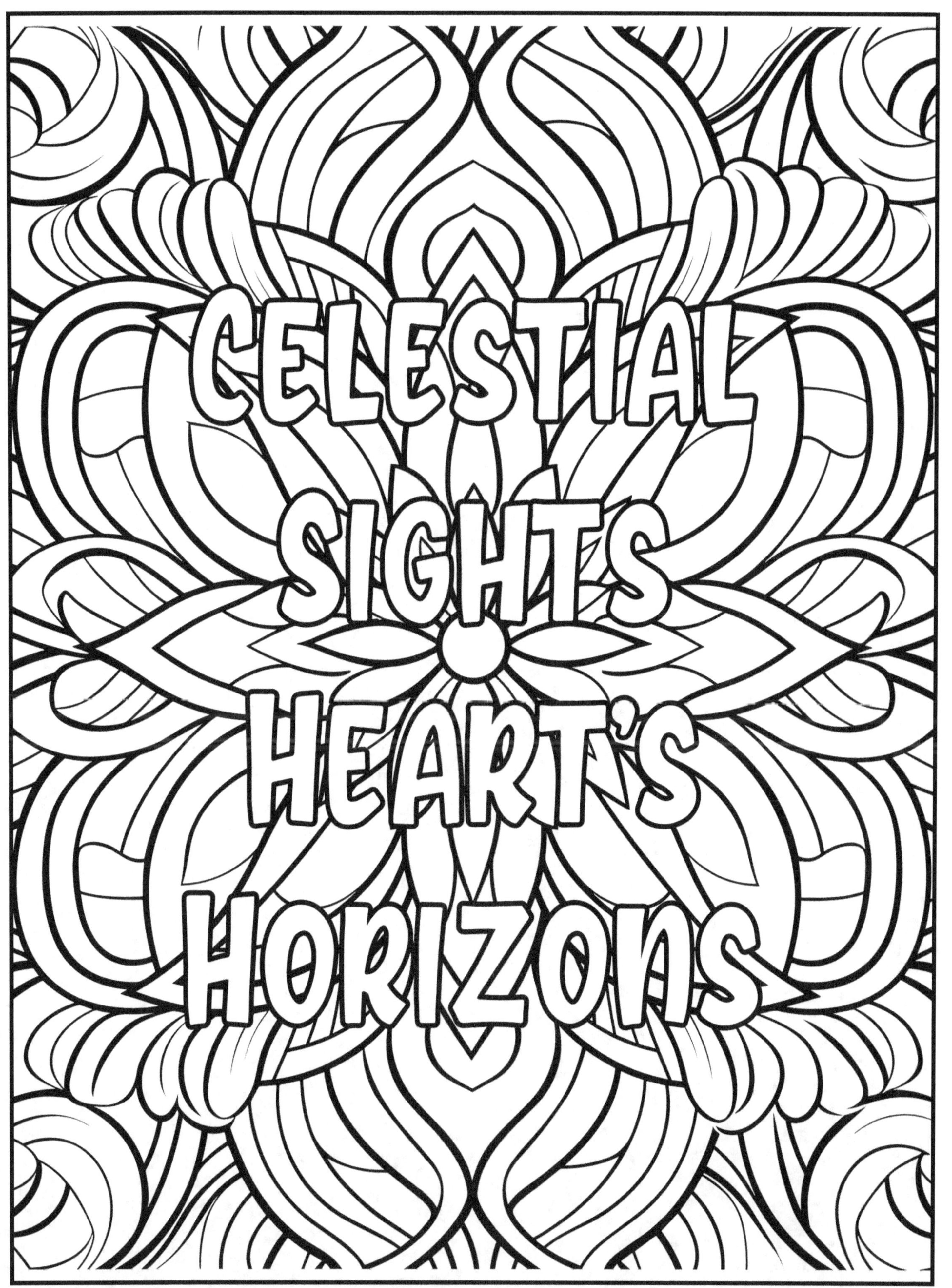

CELESTIAL
SIGHTS
HEART'S
HORIZONS

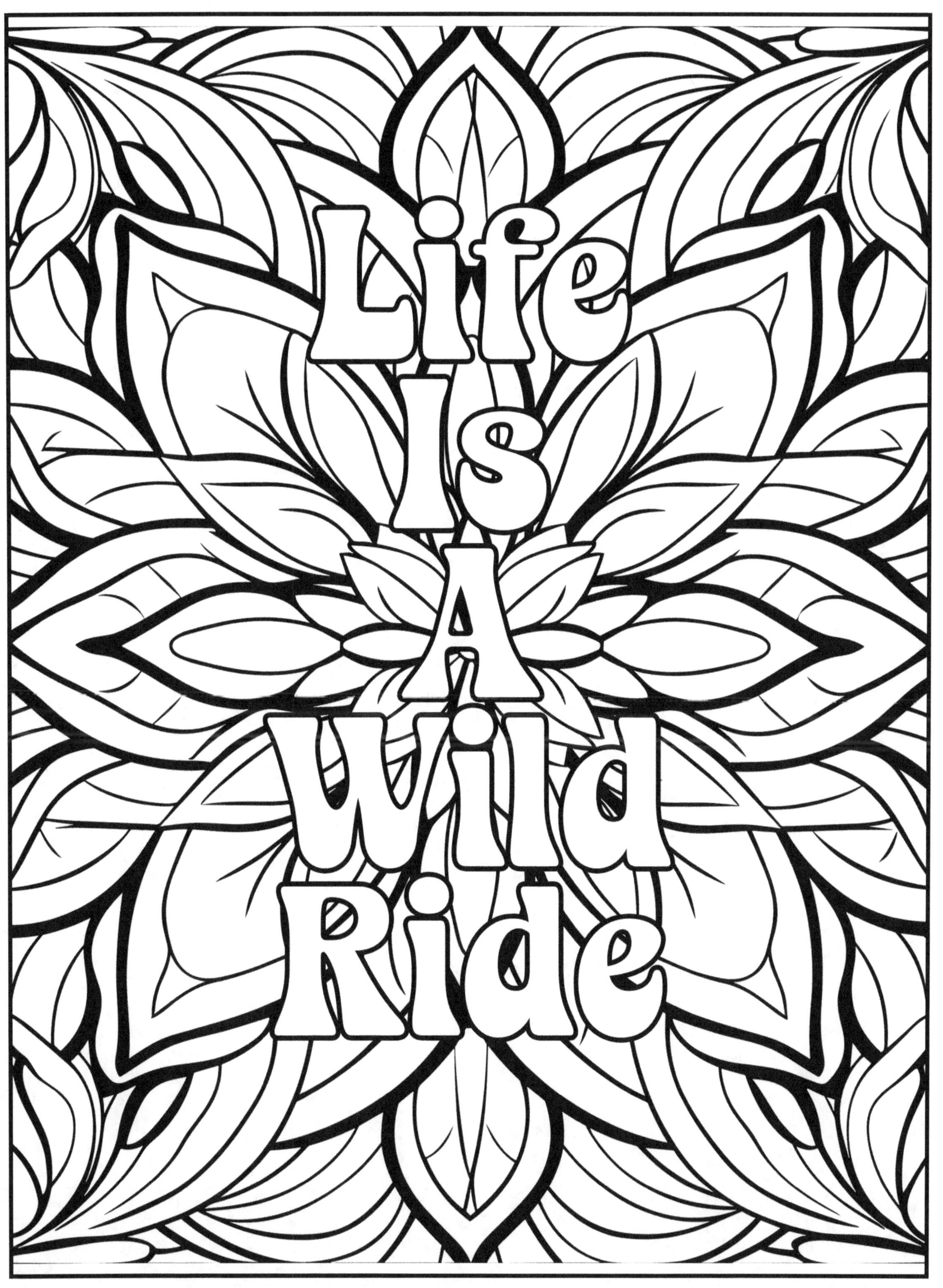

Life
is
A
Wild
Ride

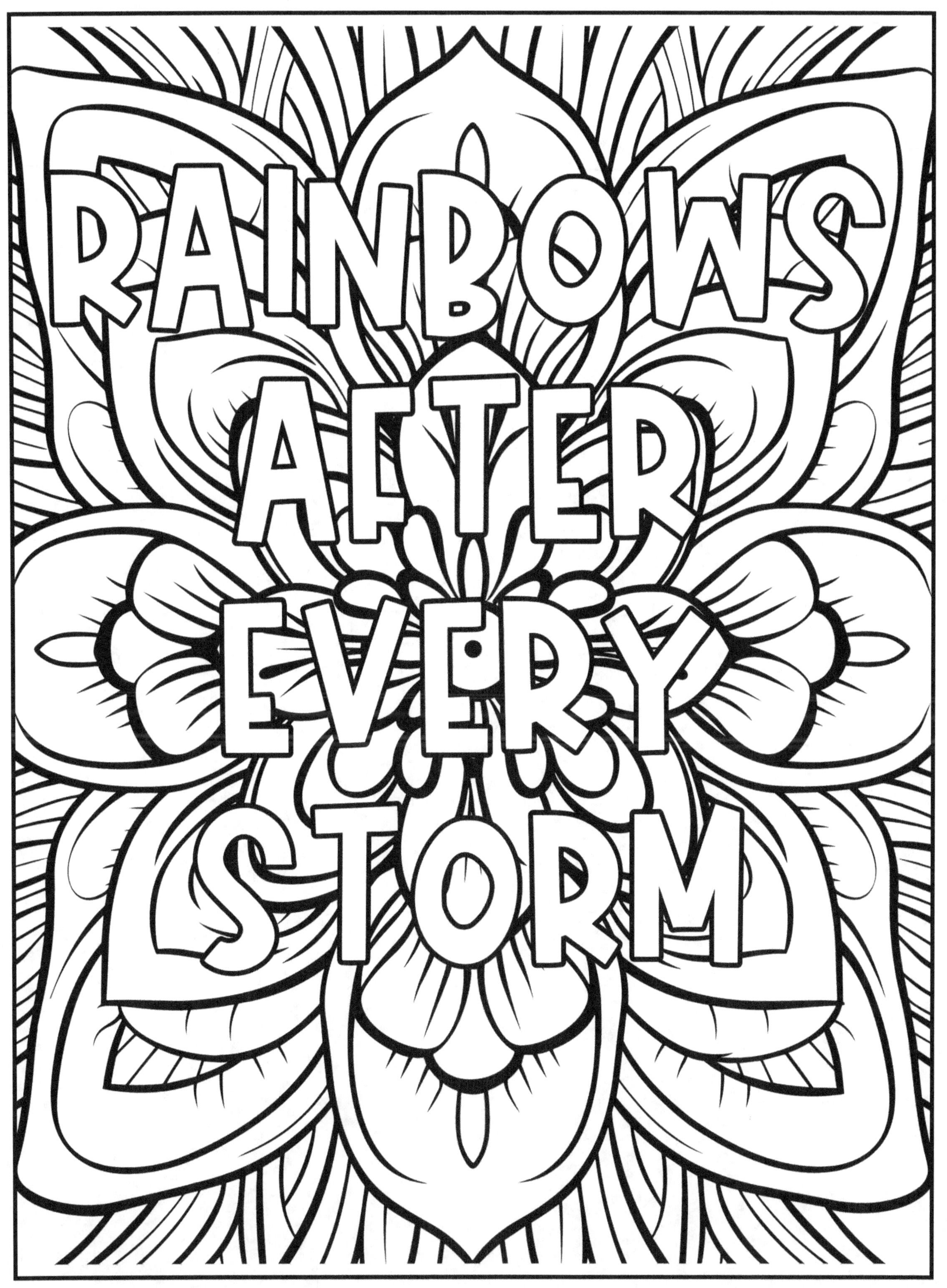
RAINBOWS AFTER EVERY STORM

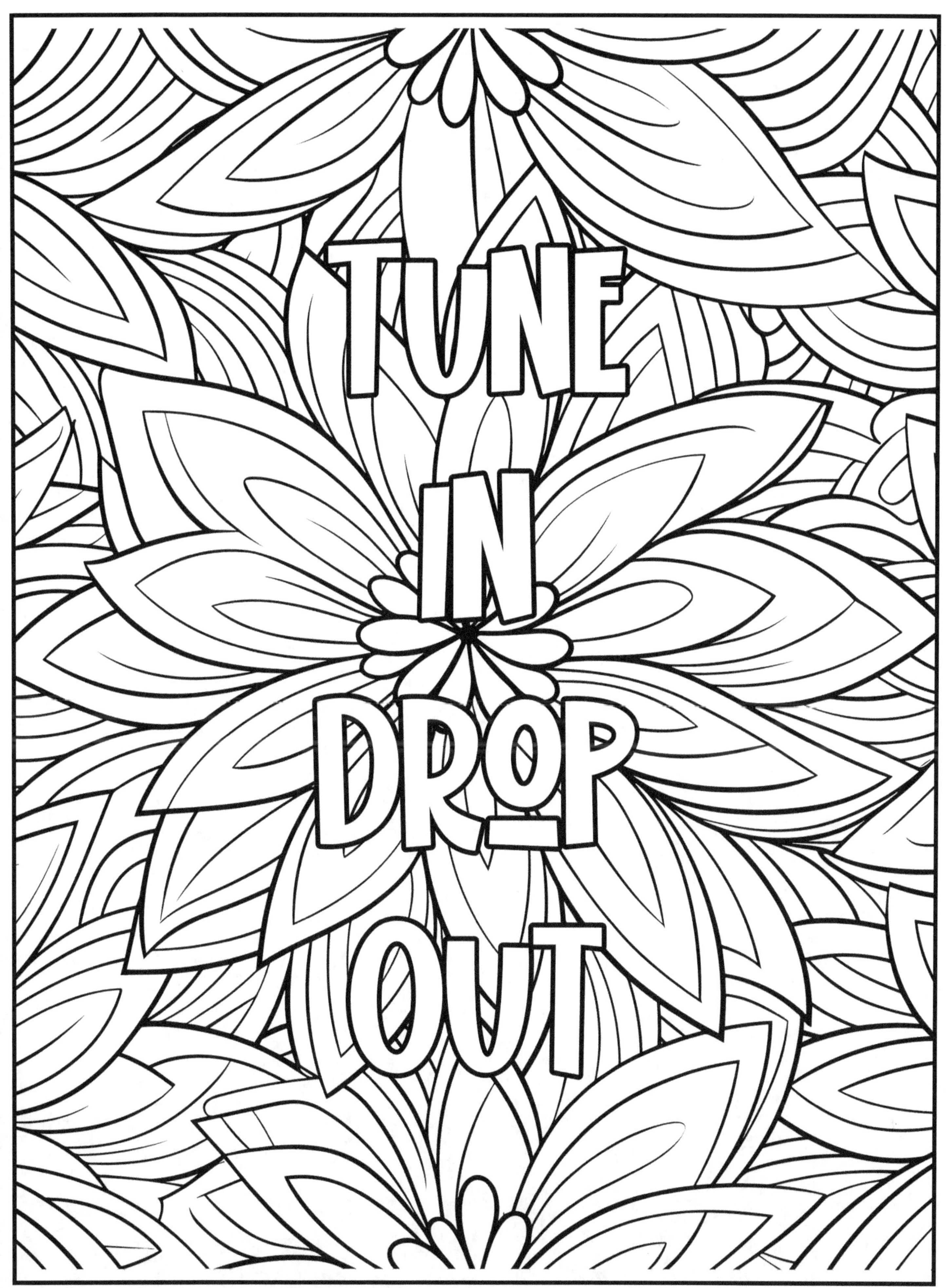
TUNE
IN
DROP
OUT

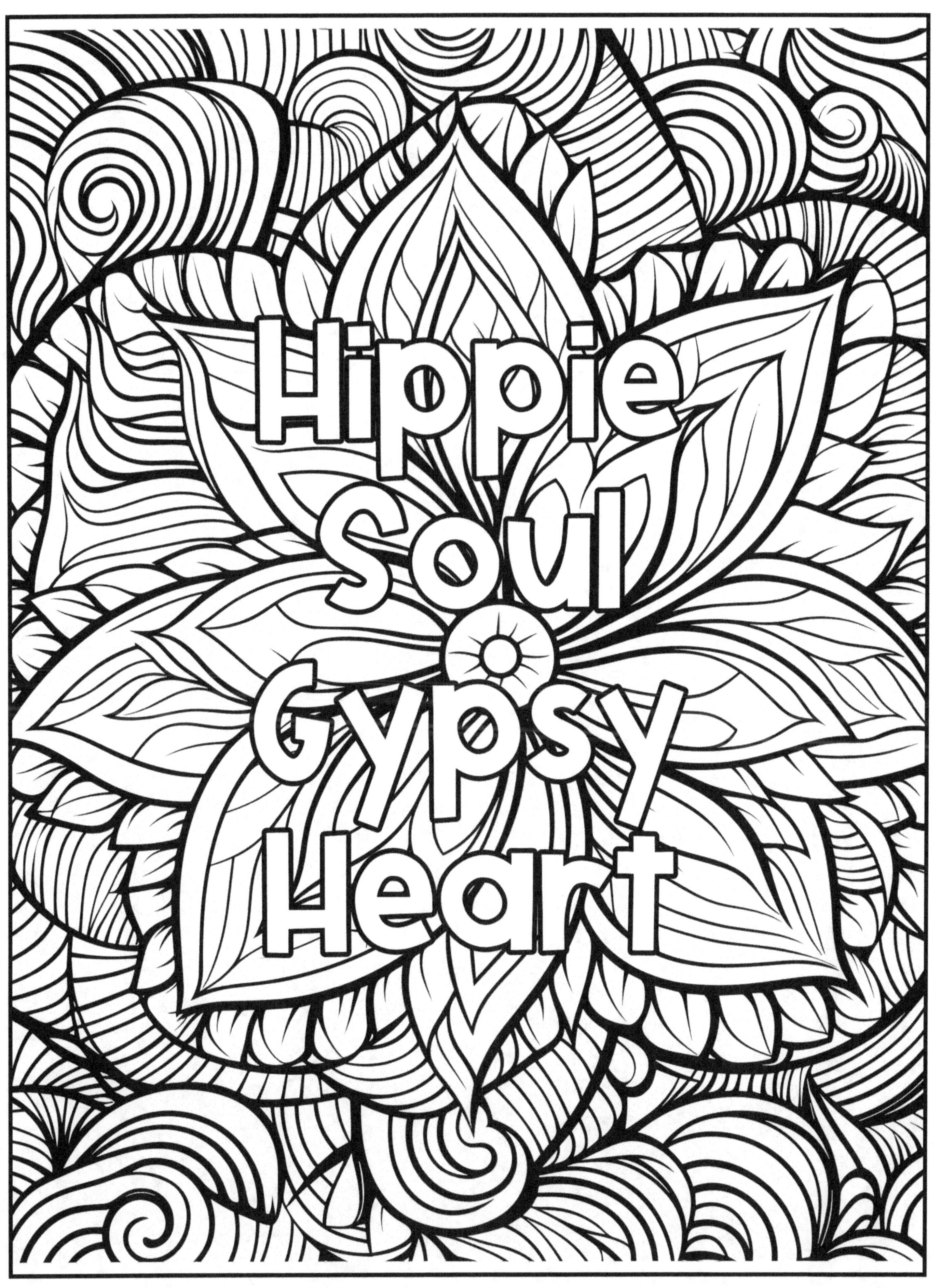

Hippie
Soul
Gypsy
Heart

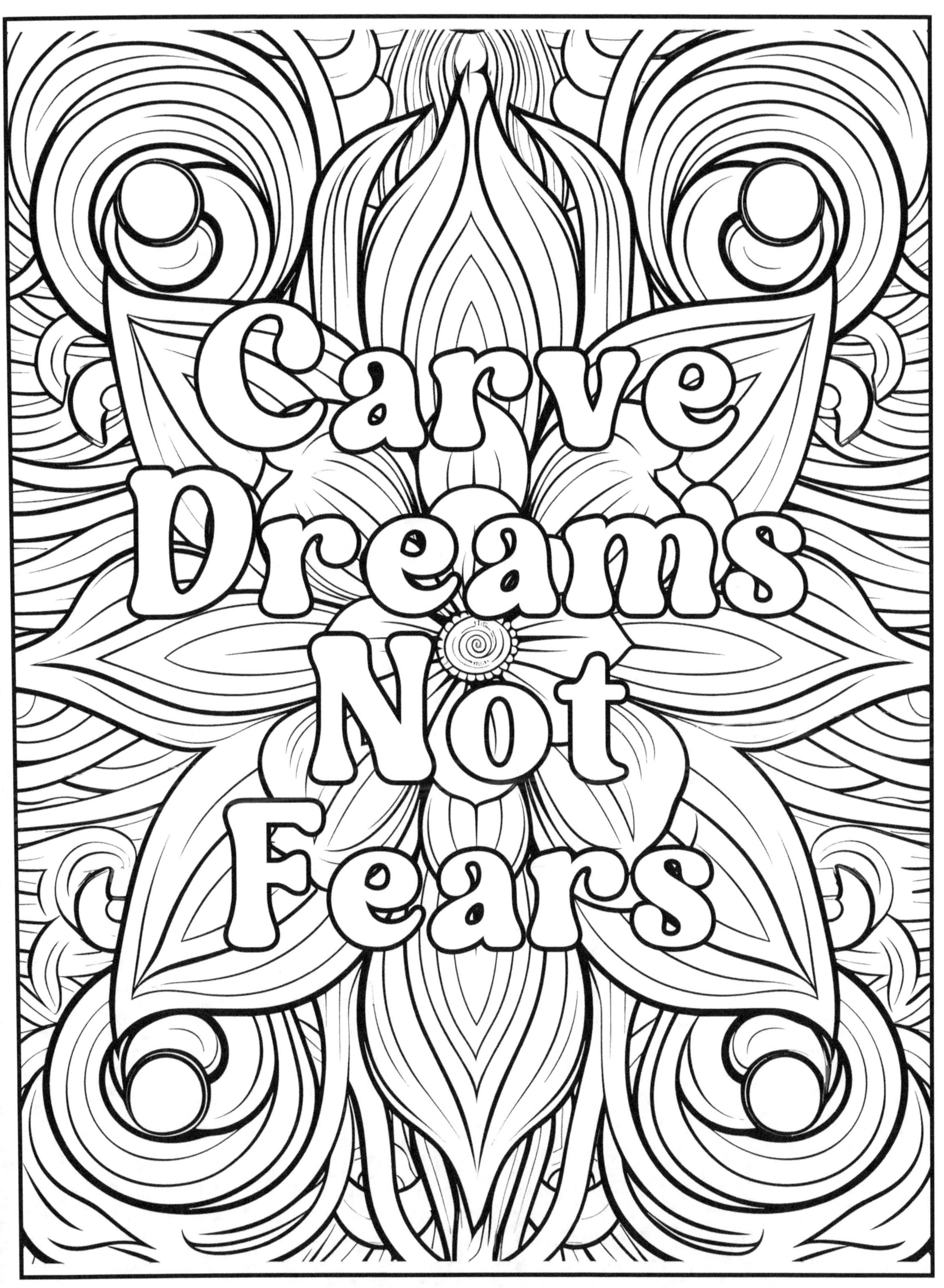

Carve
Dreams
Not
Fears

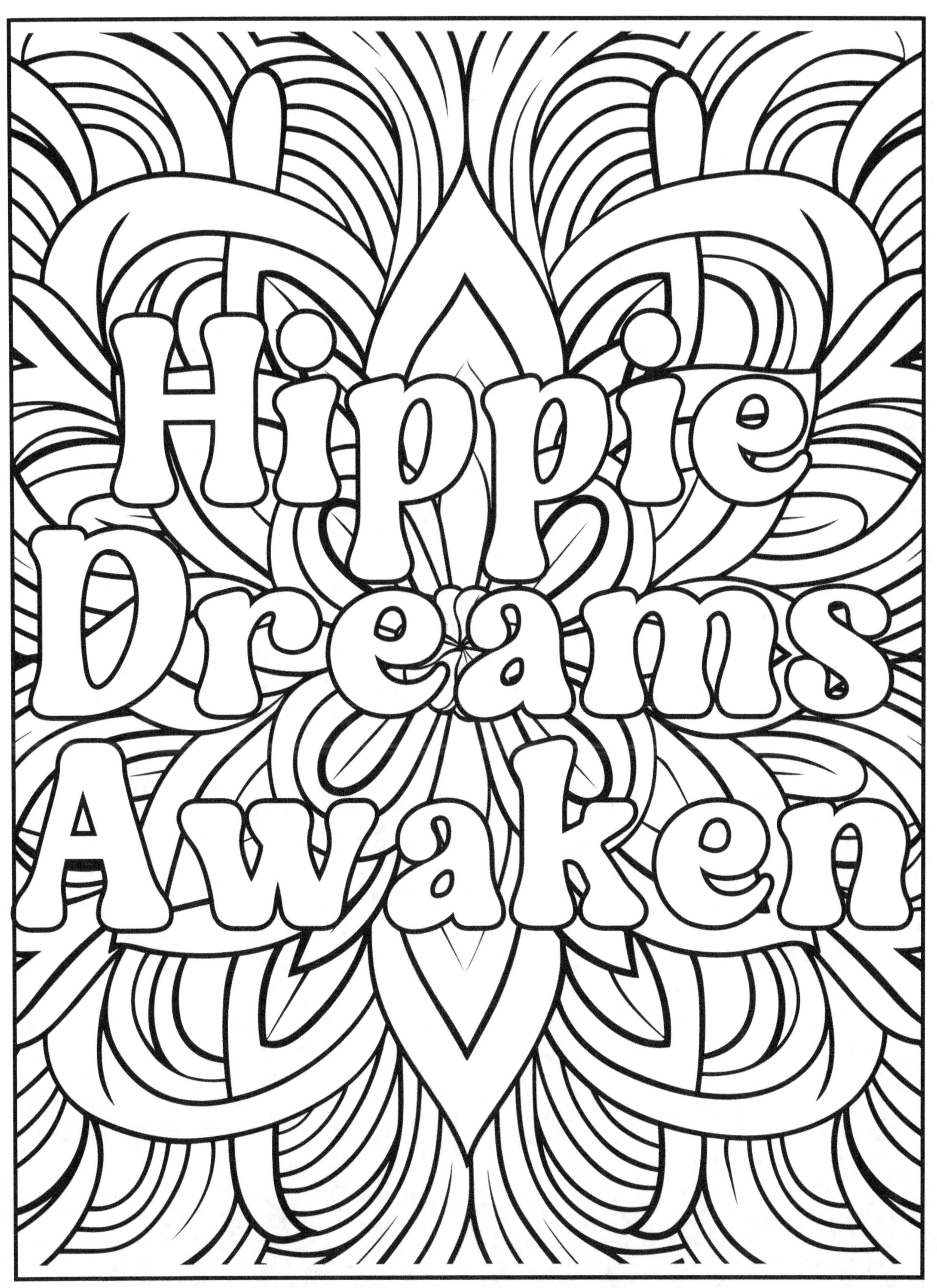

Hippie
Dreams
Awaken

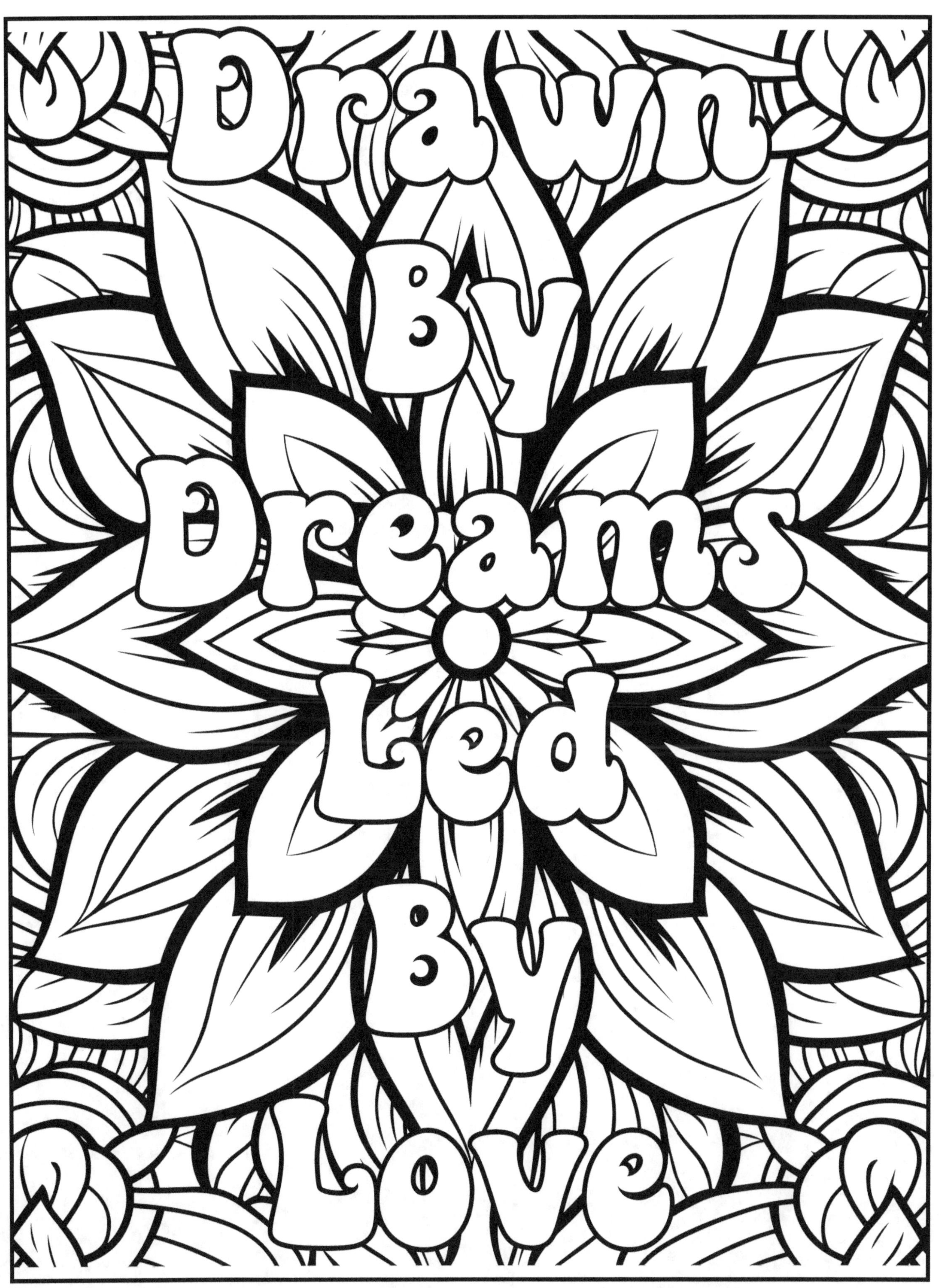

Drawn
By
Dreams
Led
By
Love

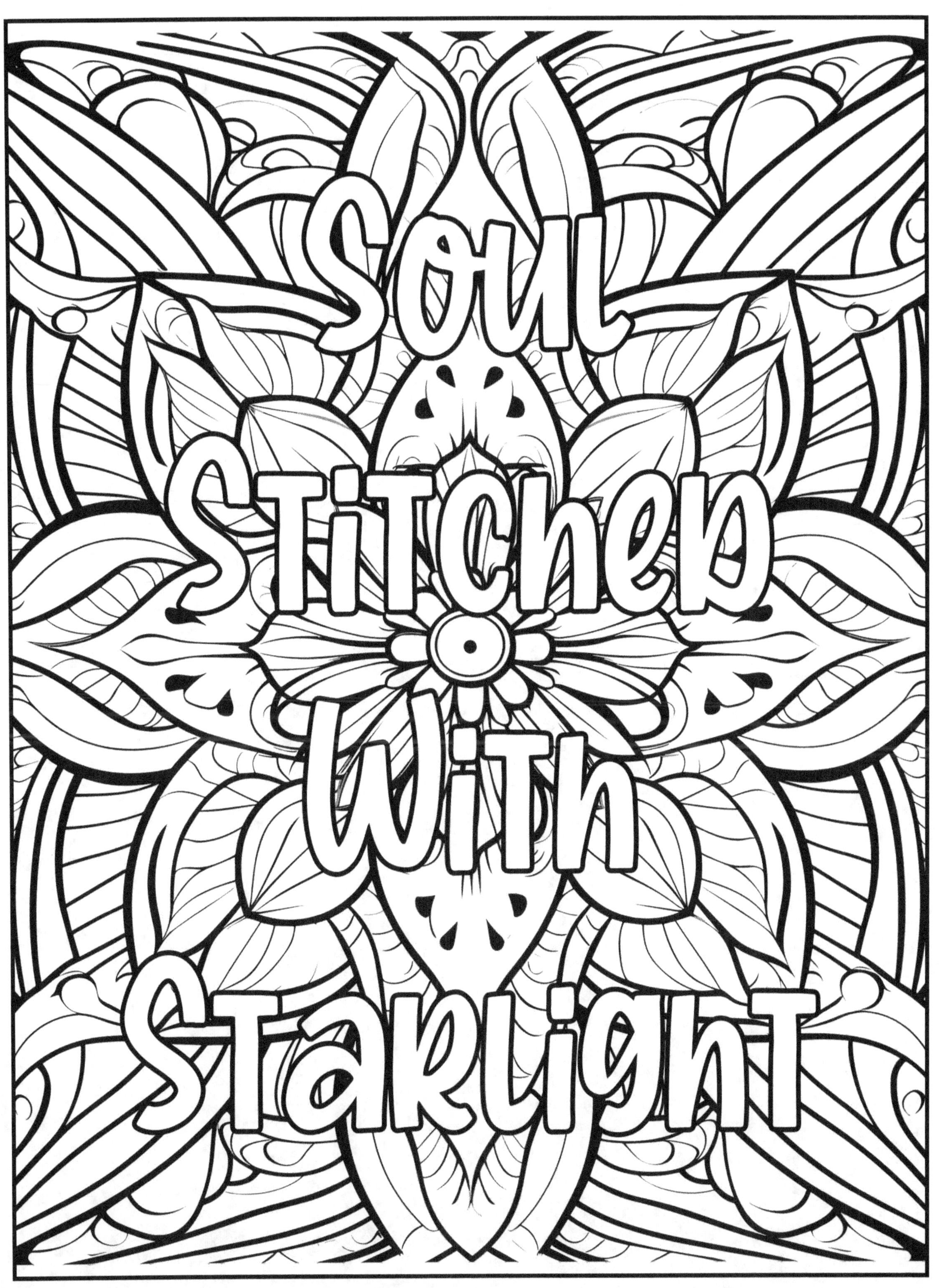

Soul
Stitched
With
Starlight

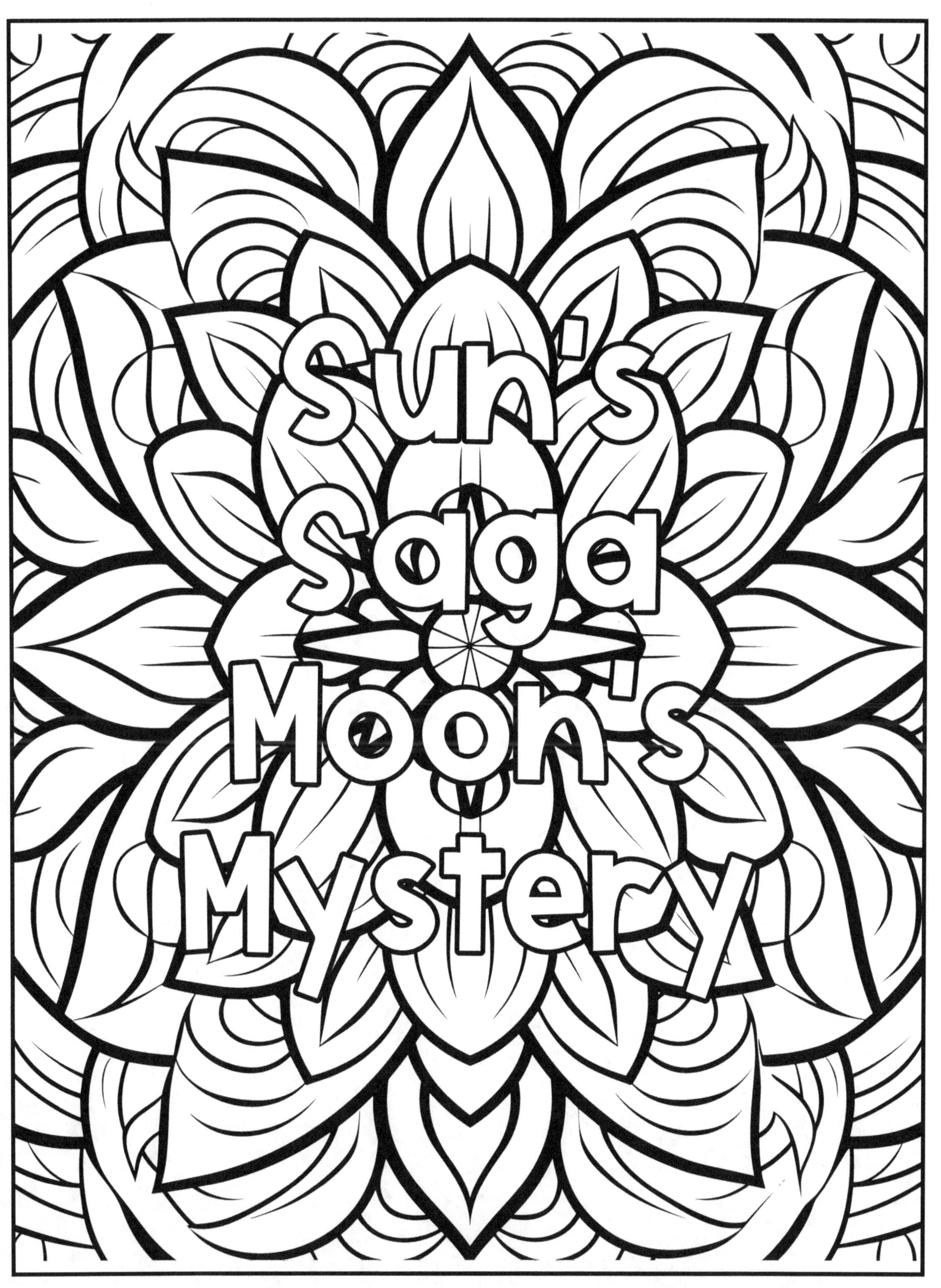

Sun's
Saga
Moon's
Mystery

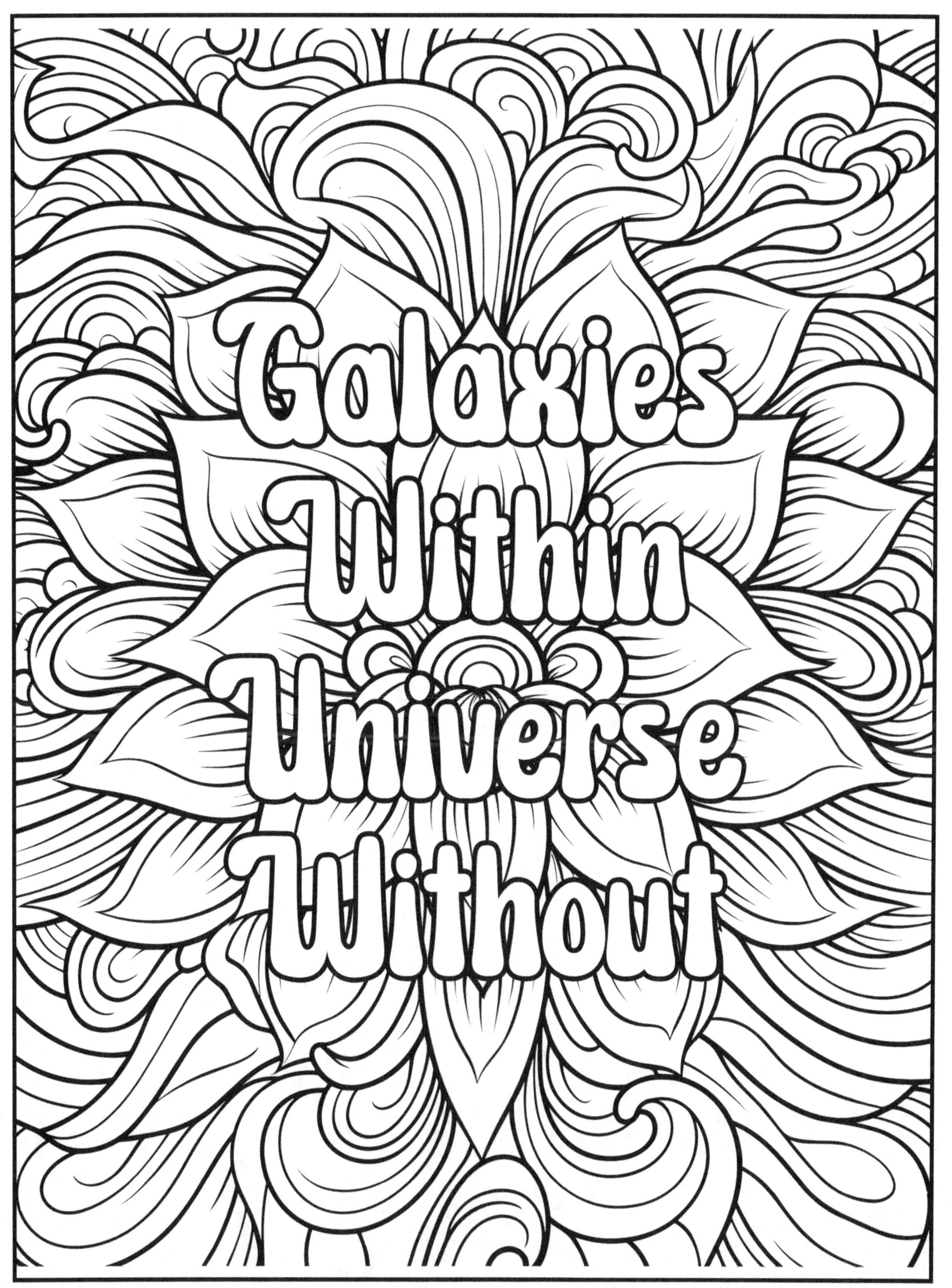

Galaxies
Within
Universe
Without

Life's
A
Cosmic
Journey

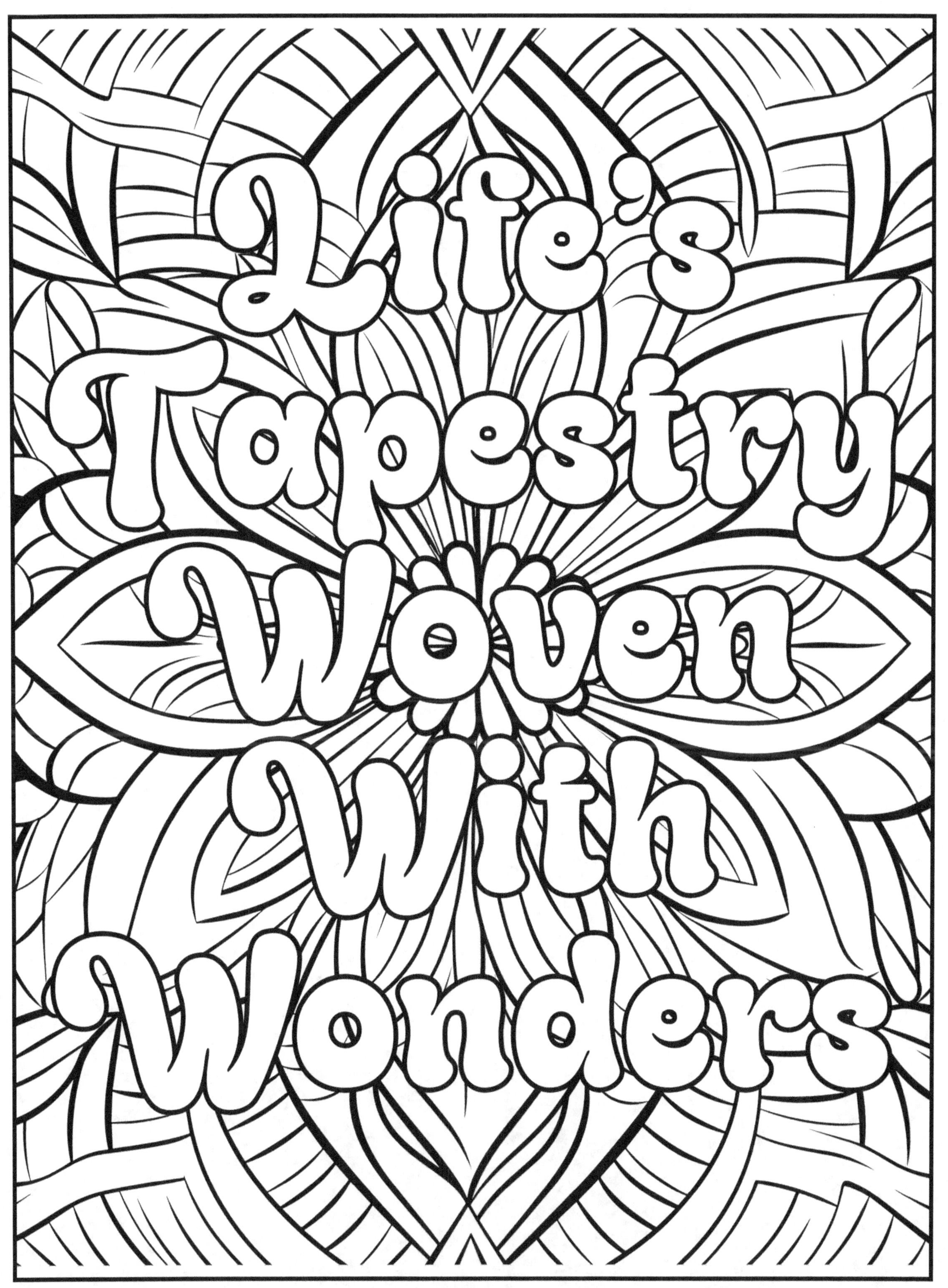

Life's
Tapestry
Woven
With
Wonders

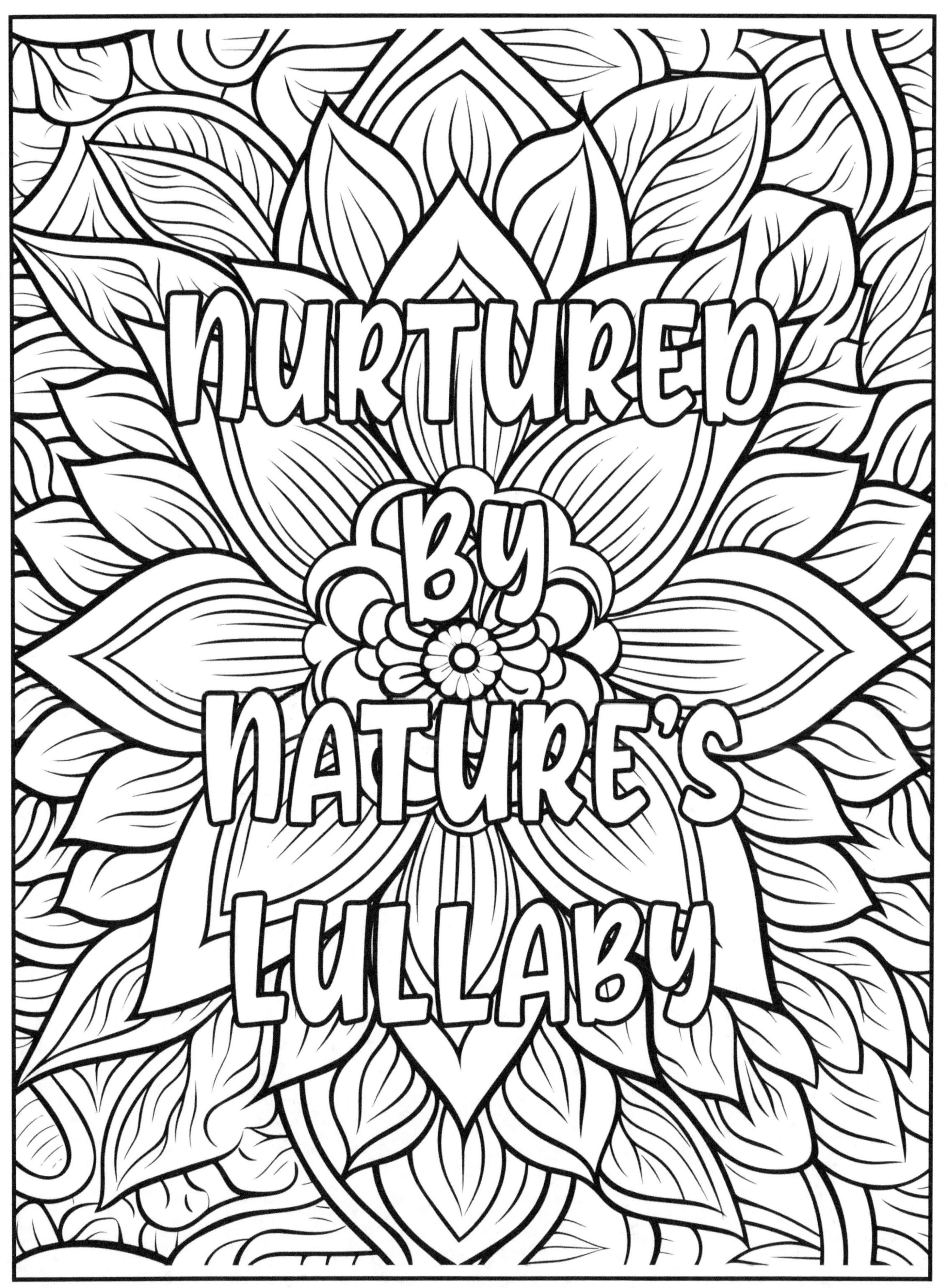

Nurtured
By
Nature's
Lullaby

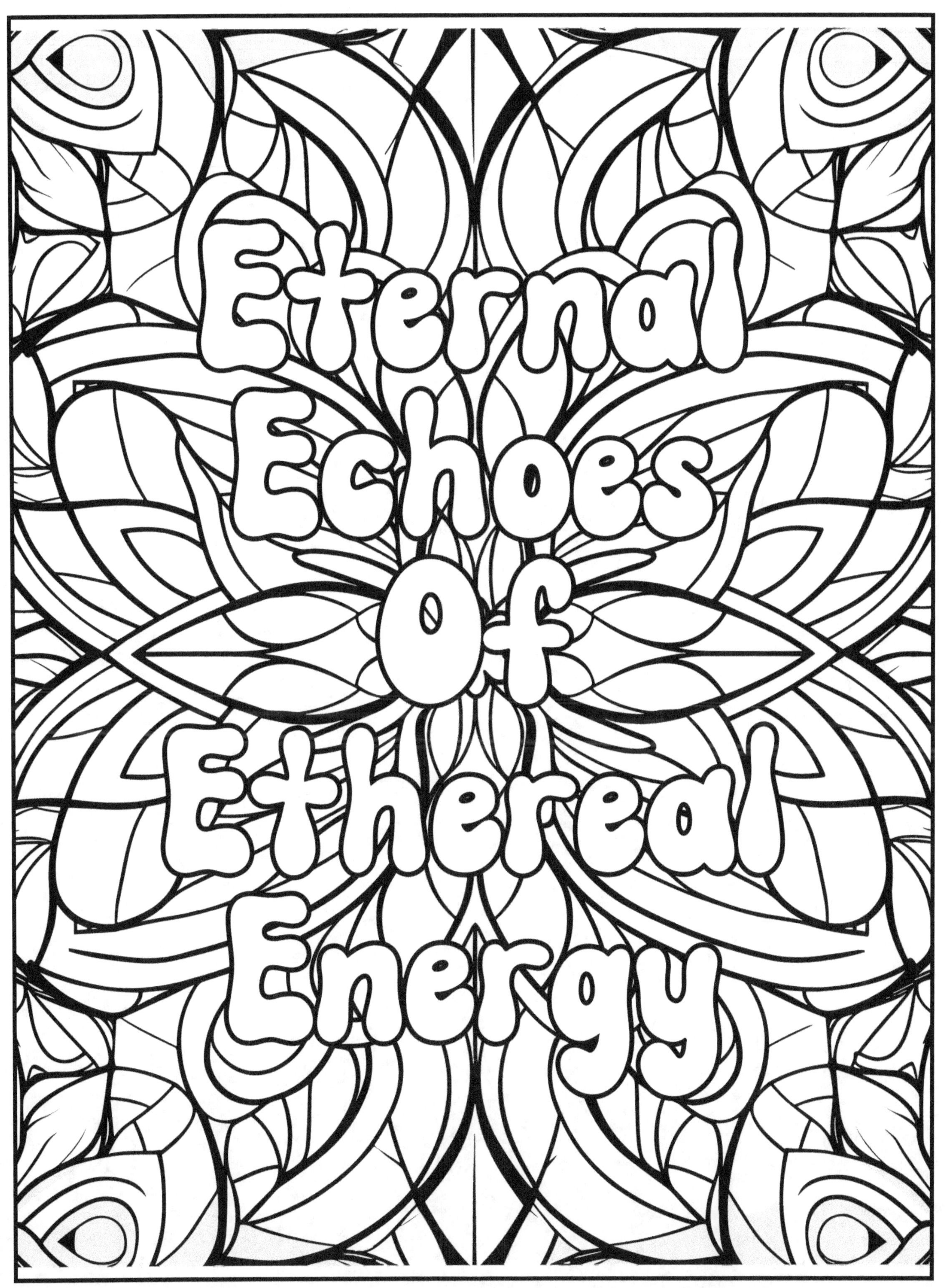

Eternal
Echoes
Of
Ethereal
Energy

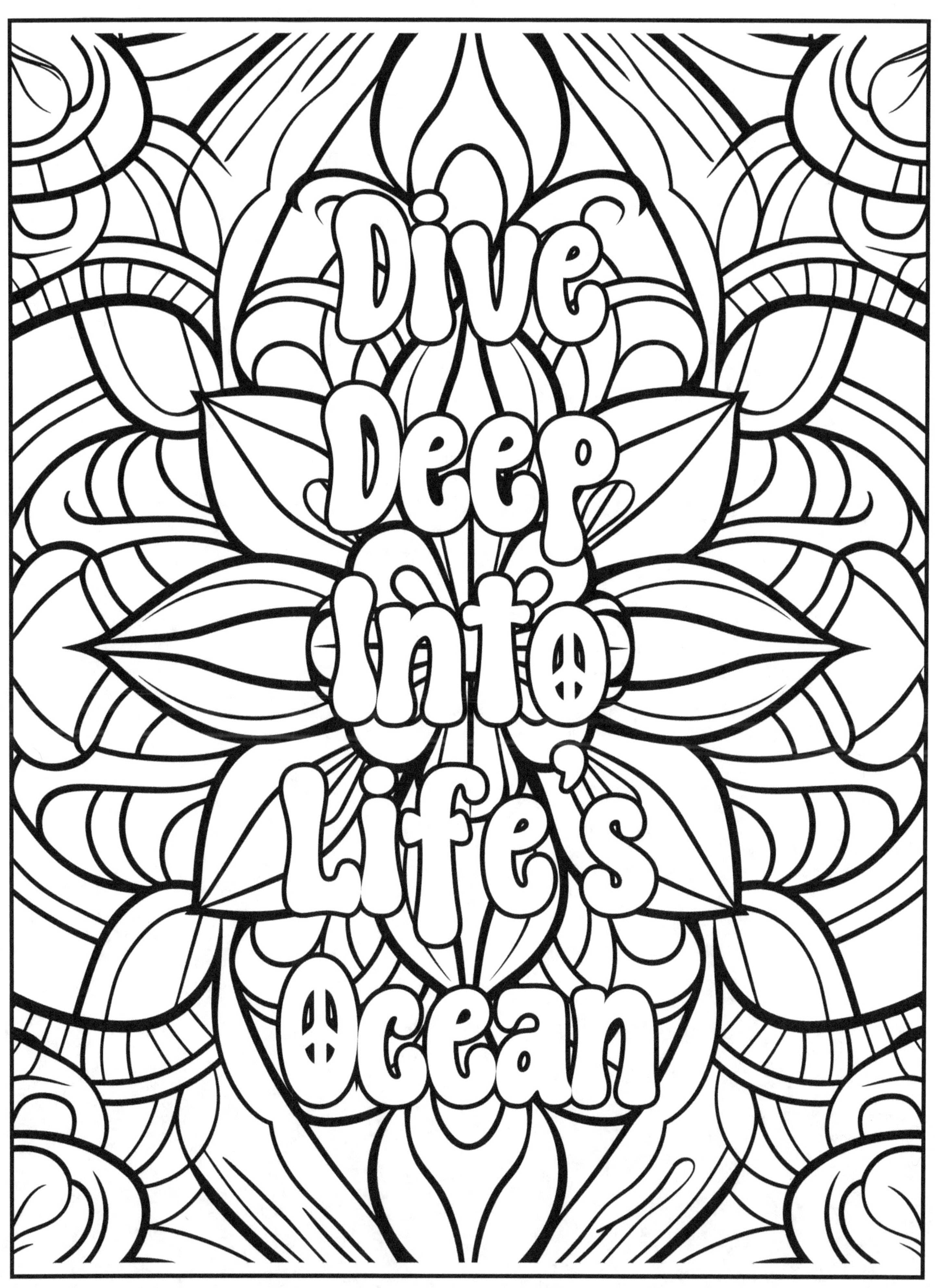

Dive
Deep
Into
Life's
Ocean

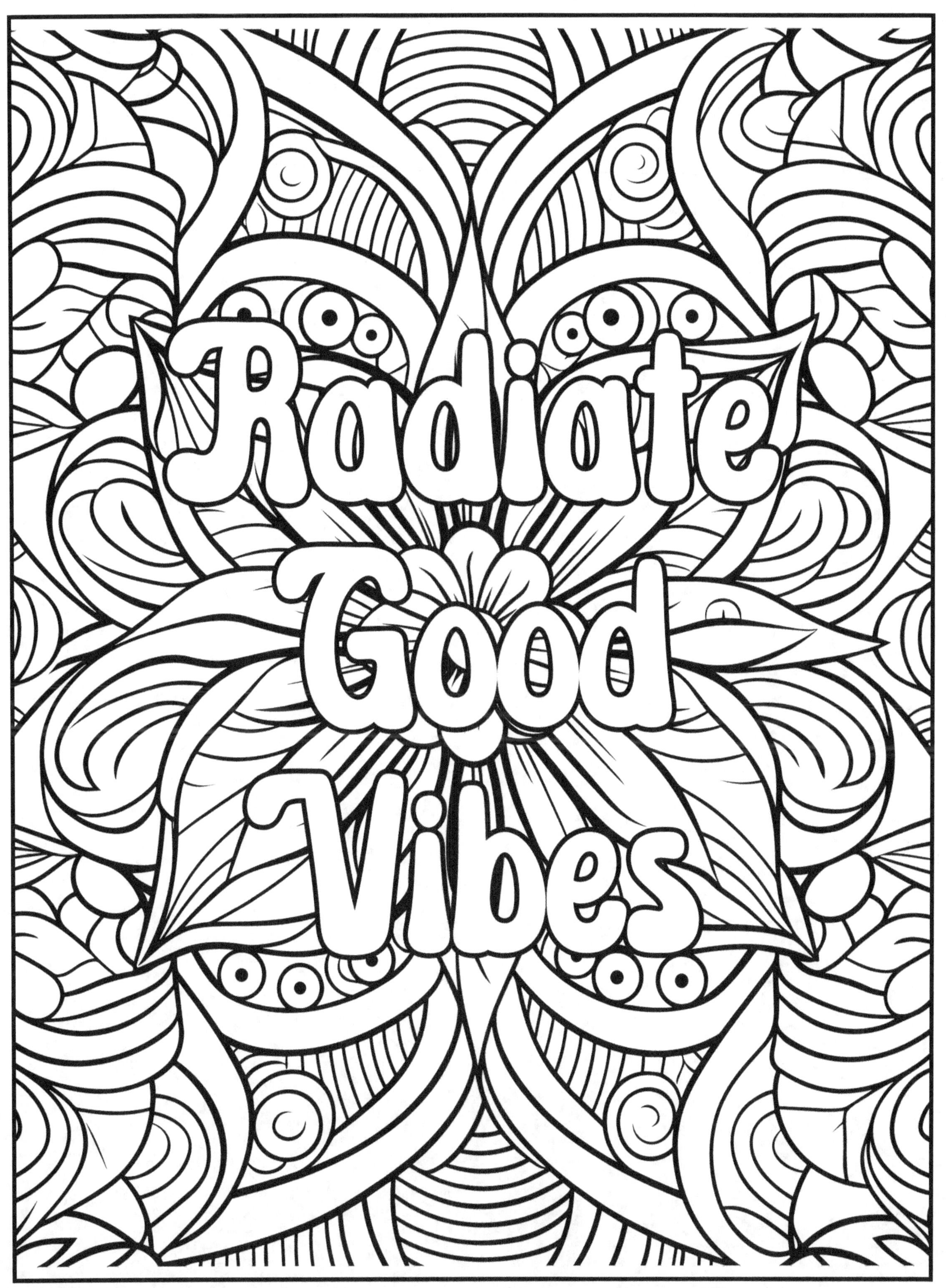

Radiate
Good
Vibes

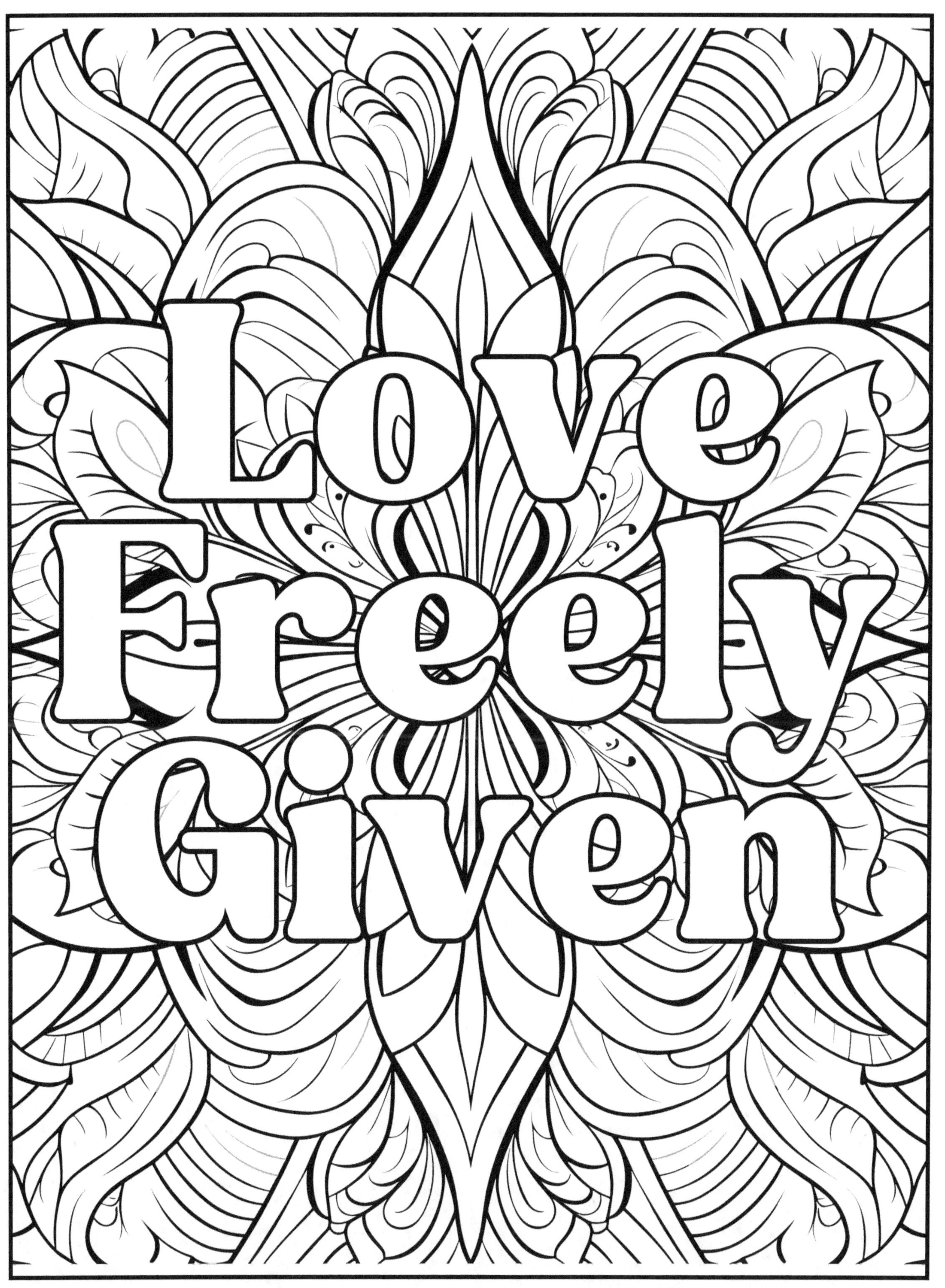

Love
Freely
Given

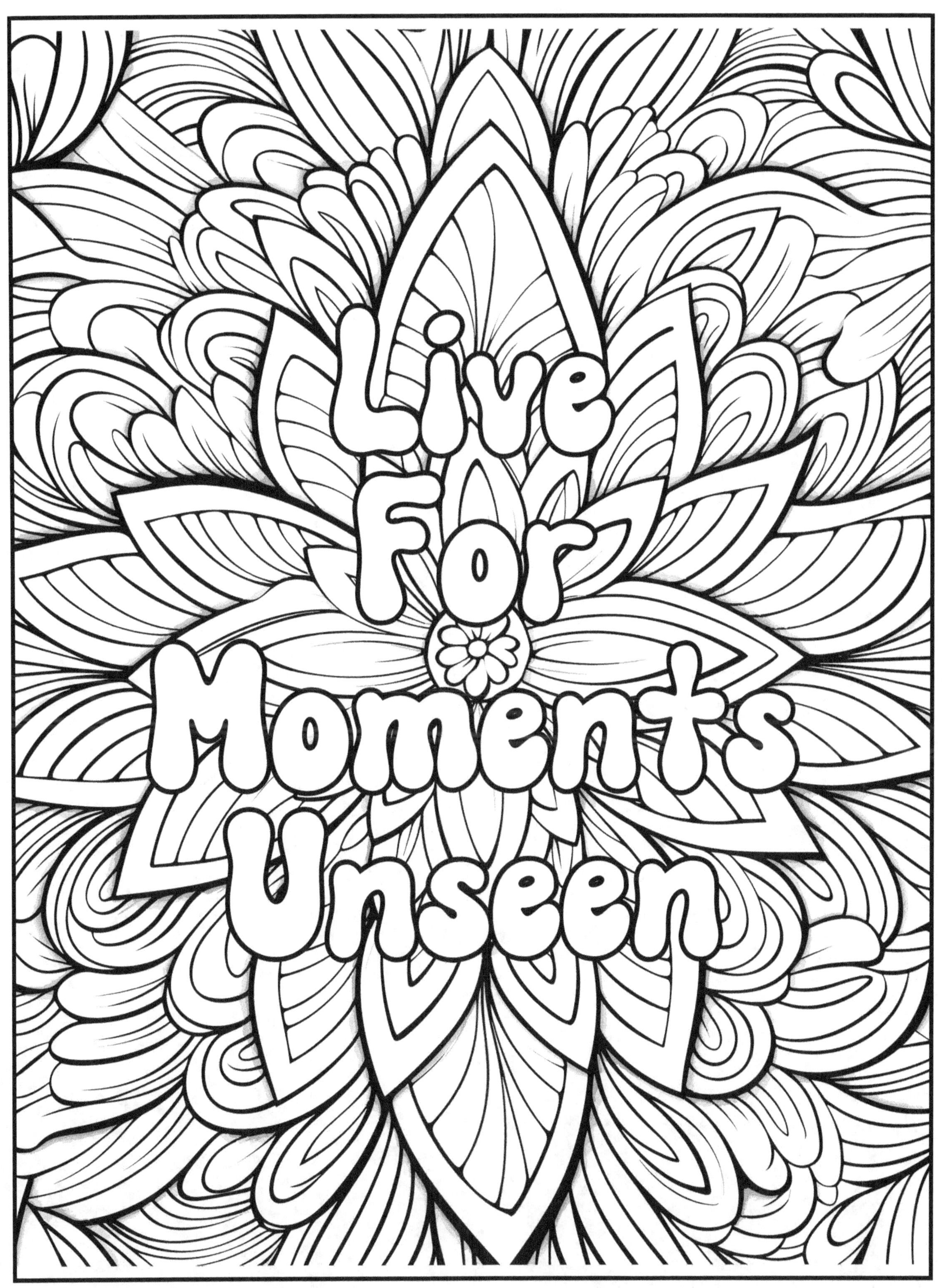

Live
For
Moments
Unseen

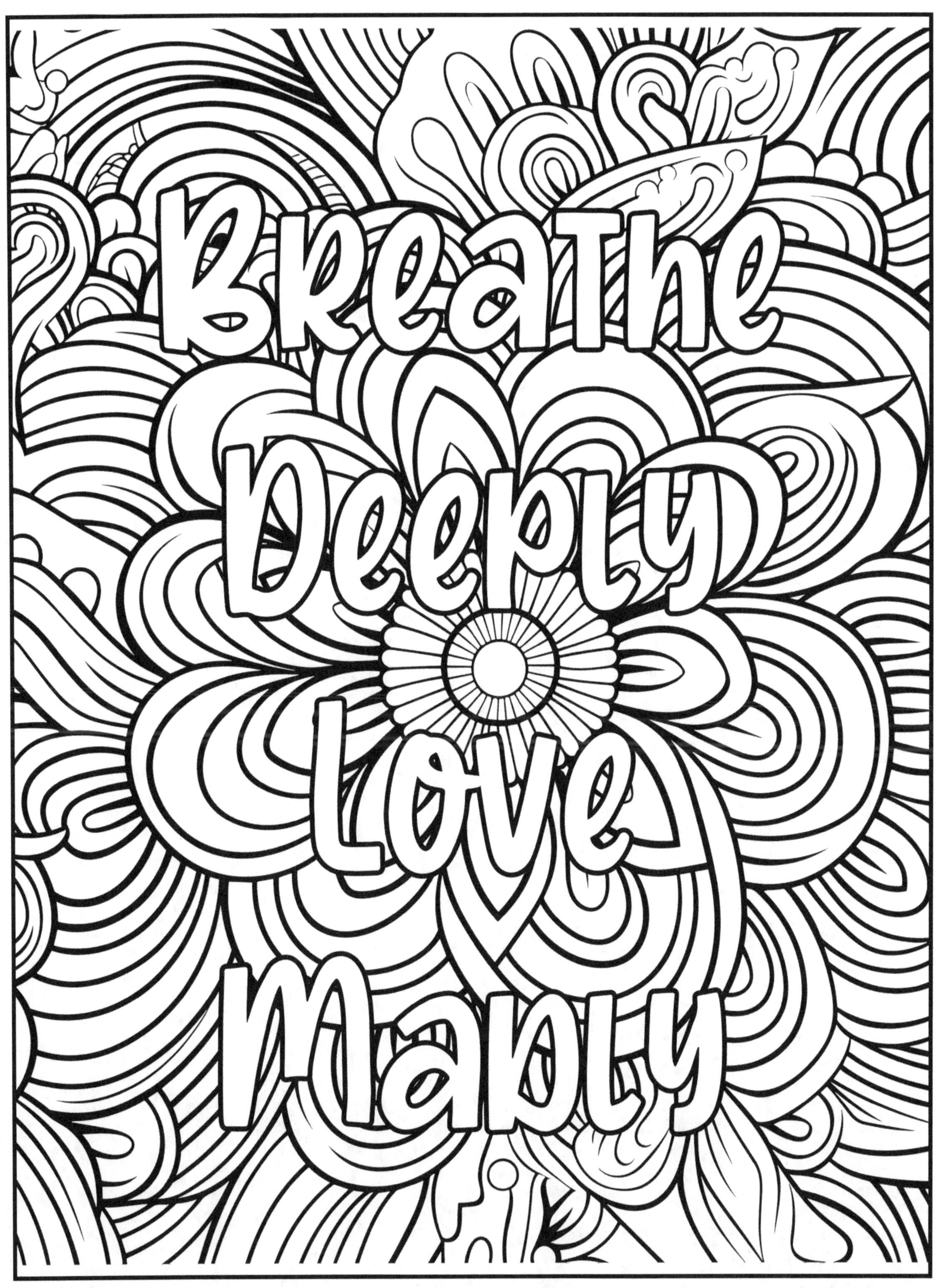
Breathe
Deeply
Love
Madly

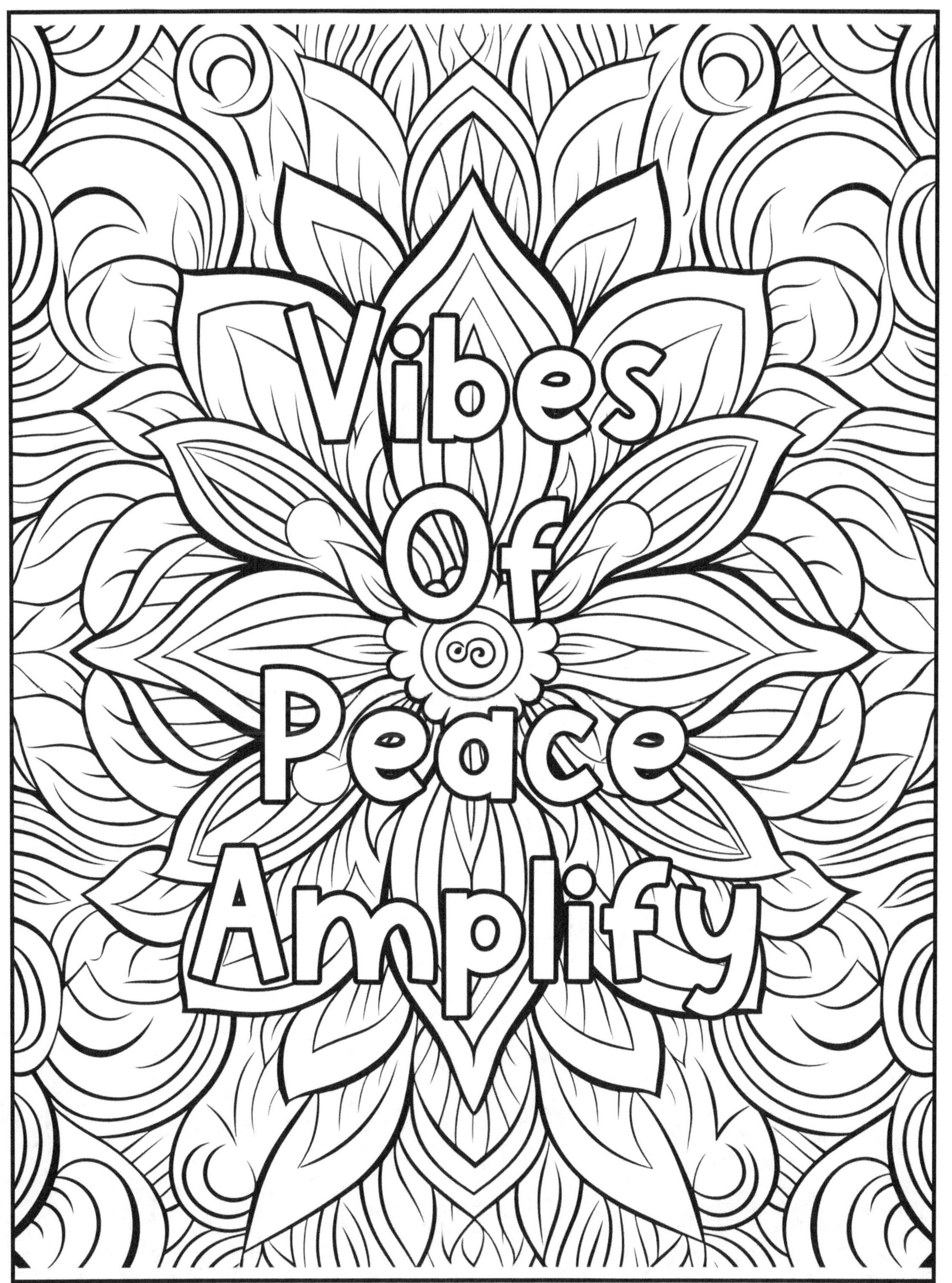

Vibes
Of
Peace
Amplify

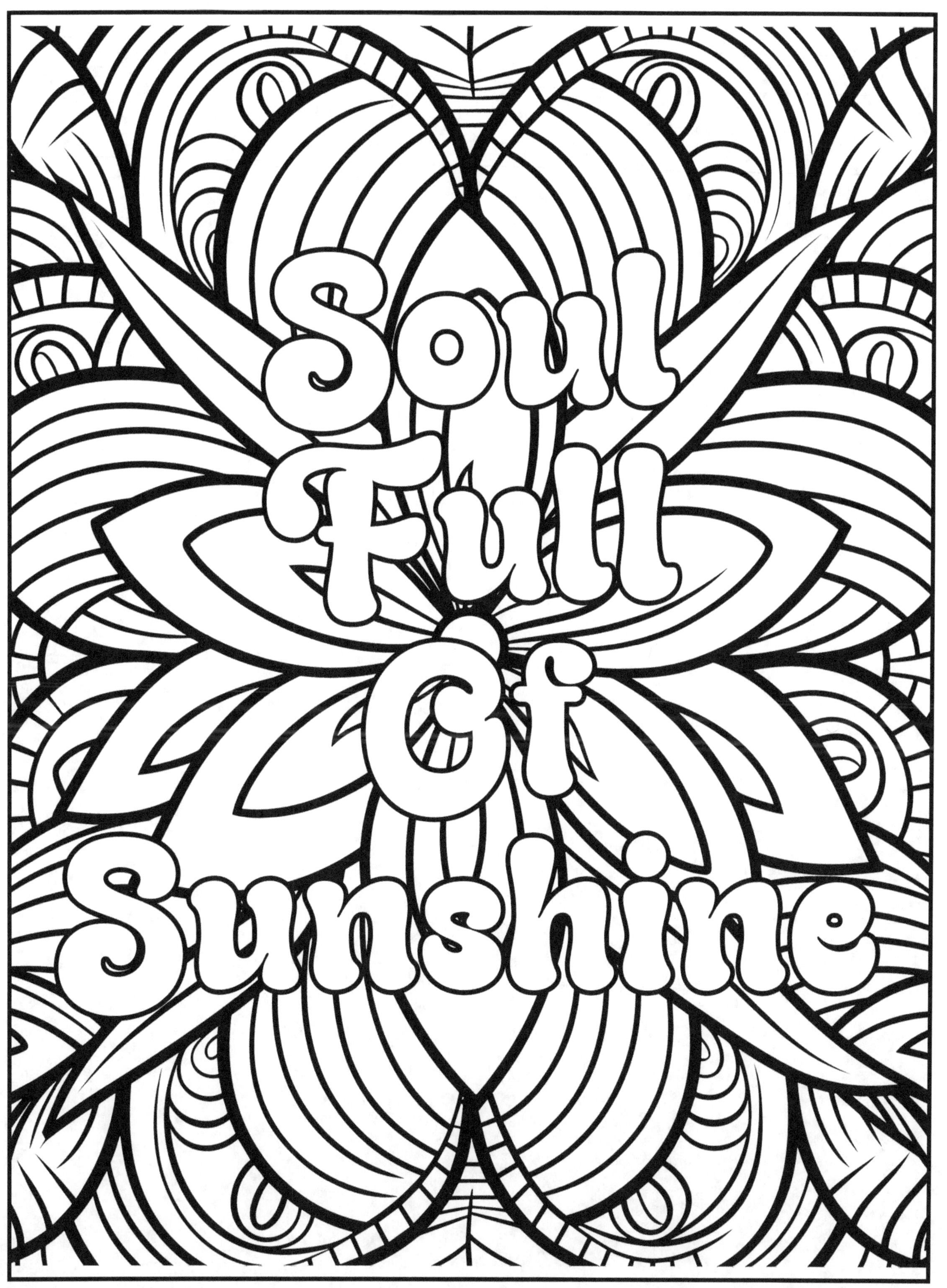

Soul
Full
Of
Sunshine

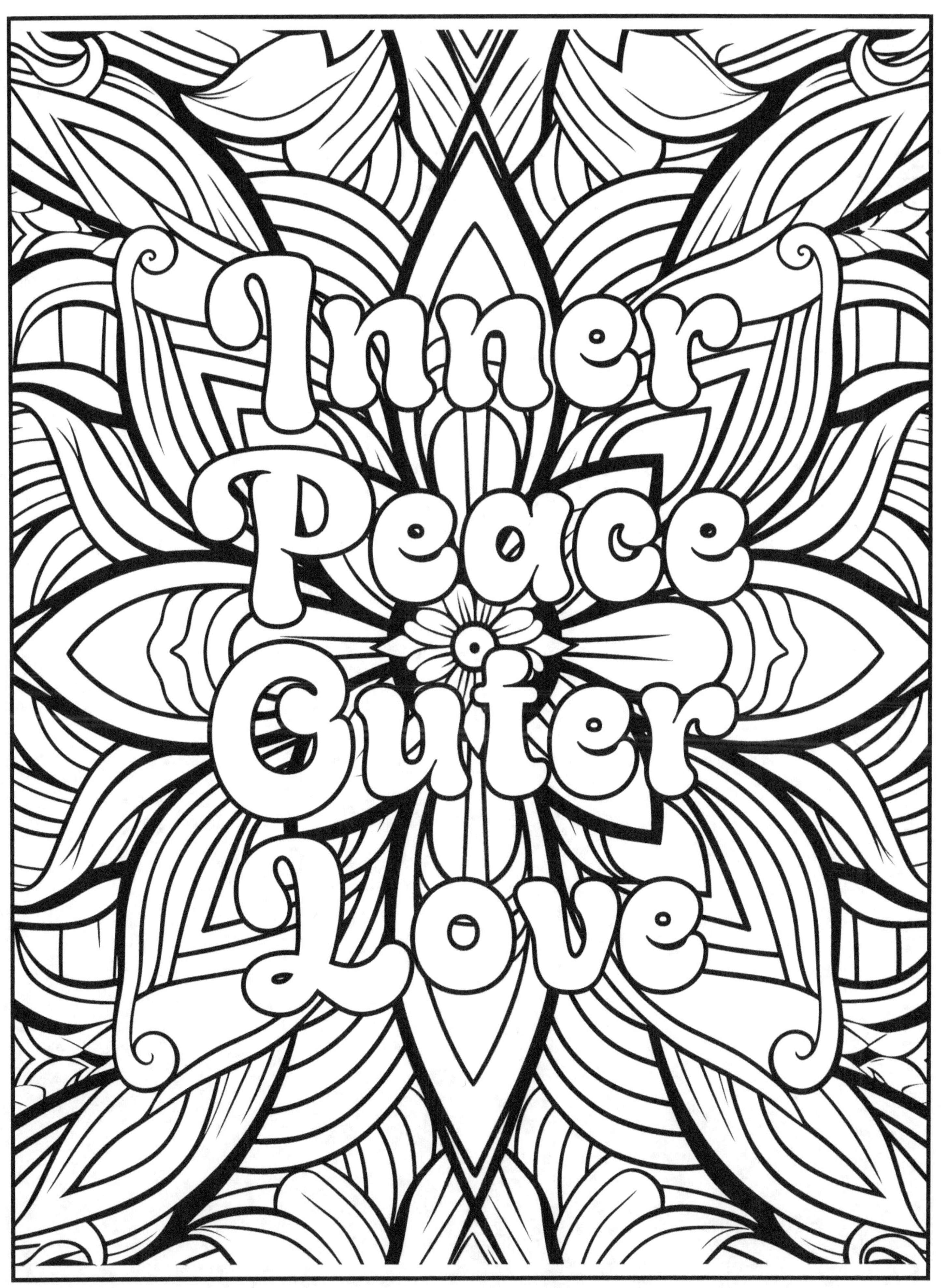

Inner
Peace
Outer
Love

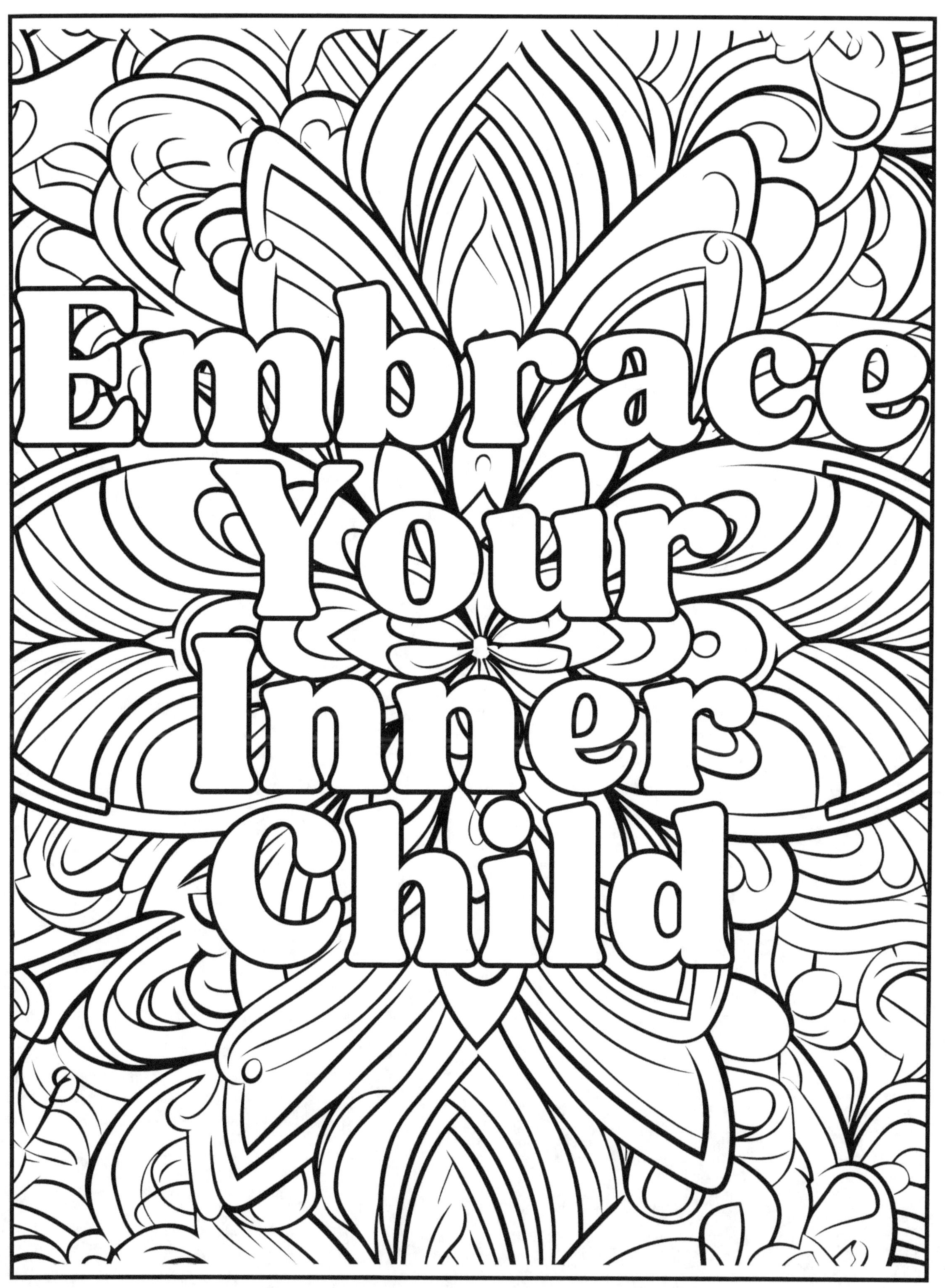
Embrace Your Inner Child

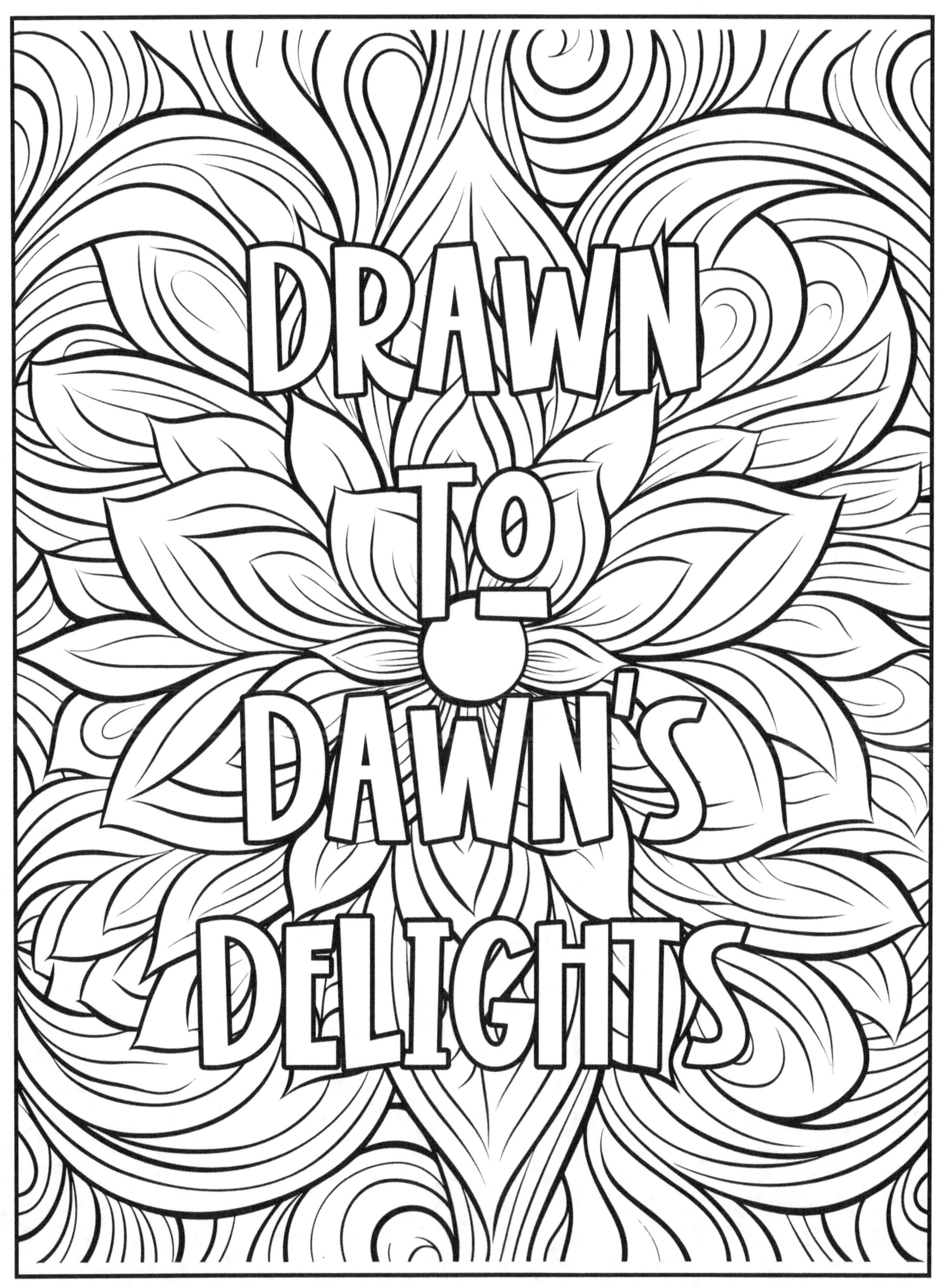
DRAWN
TO
DAWN'S
DELIGHTS

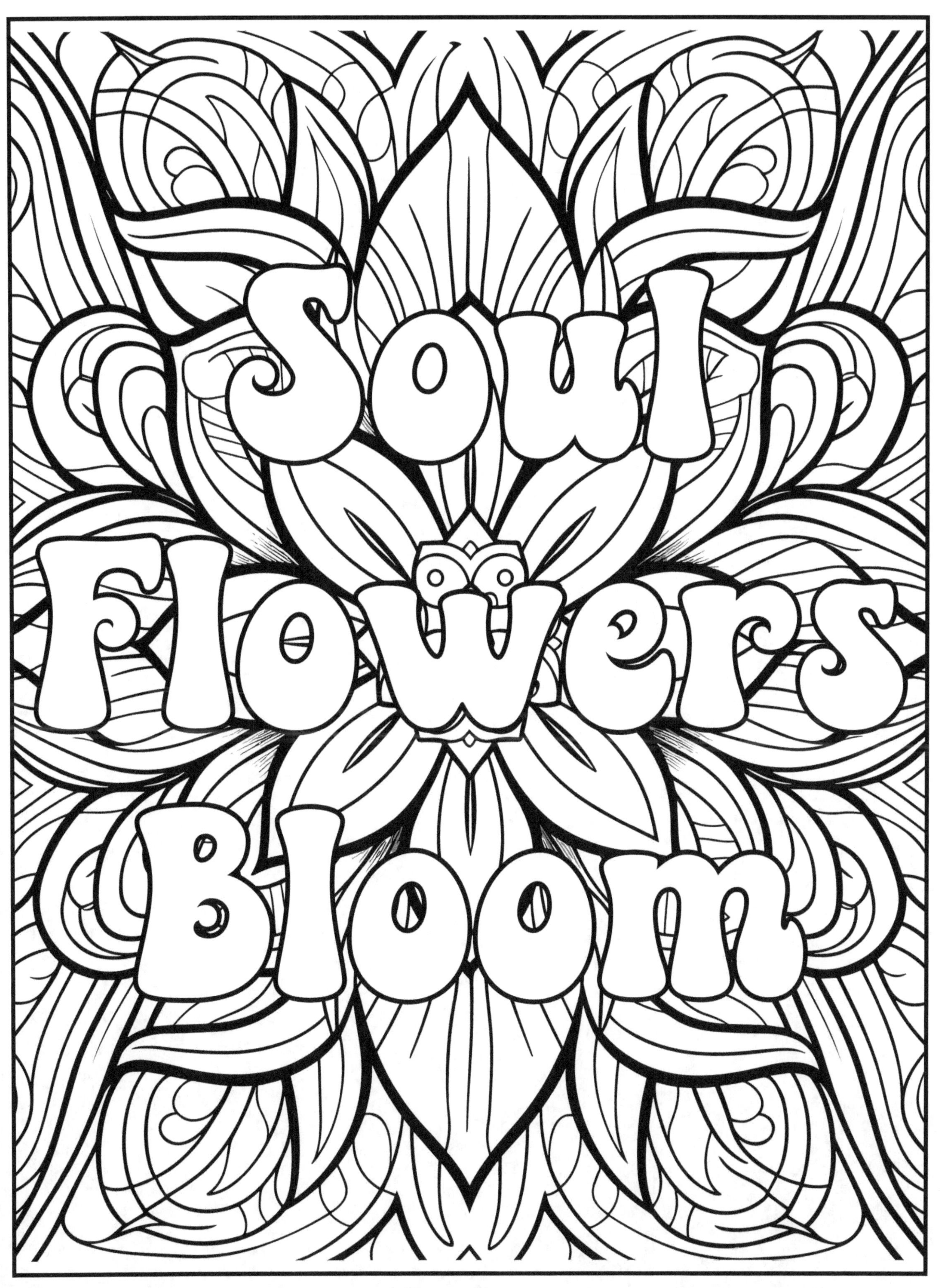

Soul
Flowers
Bloom

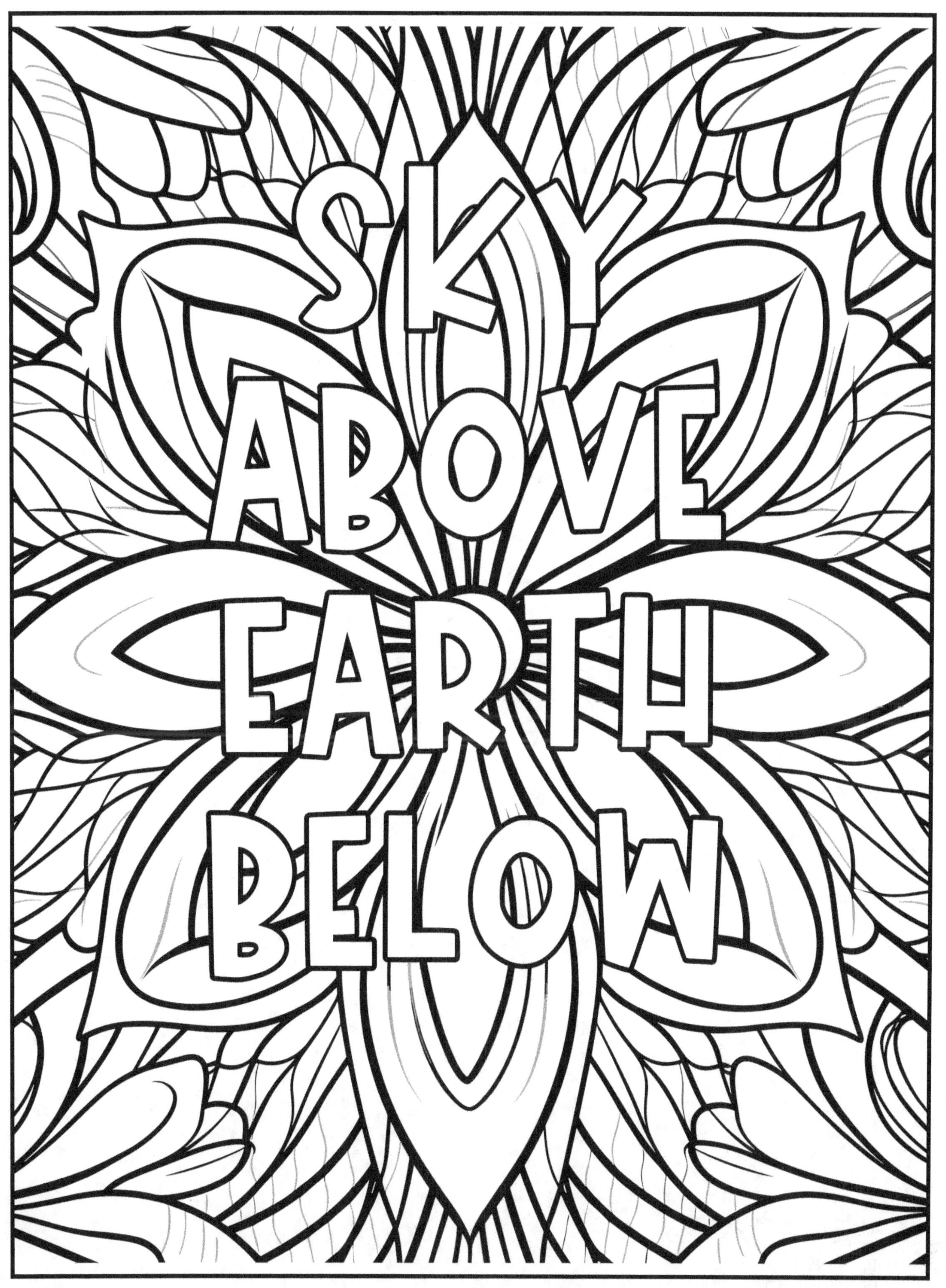

SKY
ABOVE
EARTH
BELOW